Ides

A COLLECTION OF POETRY CHAPBOOKS

Ides

A Collection of Poetry Chapbooks

Edited by
Melanie Villines

Art by
Amedeo Modigliani

SILVER BIRCH PRESS
LOS ANGELES, CALIFORNIA

© Copyright 2015, Silver Birch Press

ISBN-13: 978-0692546468

ISBN-10: 0692546464

FIRST EDITION: October 15, 2015

EMAIL: silver@silverbirchpress.com

WEB: silverbirchpress.com

BLOG: silverbirchpress.wordpress.com

MAILING ADDRESS:
Silver Birch Press
P.O. Box 29458
Los Angeles, CA 90029

COVER ART: "Woman's Head" by Amedeo Modigliani (1915).

Interior Art by Amedeo Modigliani (1884-1920).

Foreword

Silver Birch Press decided to celebrate the year 2015 by asking 15 poets to each contribute 15 pages of poetry to a chapbook collection, which we've entitled *Ides*. The result is a diverse mix of poetry by authors from coast to coast. Our poets hail from California, Florida, Illinois, Maine, Massachusetts, New Jersey, New York, the Carolinas, and Texas—with one from Canada. We hope you enjoy their eclectic collections.

As art, we've selected paintings by Amedeo Modigliani—primarily work he created in his prolific year of 1915. A century later, we celebrate him as a visionary artist who accomplished much in his very short life.

A special thank you to the poets whose work appears in these pages. We applaud your dedication to the art and craft of poetry.

Contents

Ides

Good Woman Gone

Jeffrey C. Alfier

When will kindness have such power again?
— EDMUND BLUNDEN

Jezebel Drafts a Dispatch to Ahab on the End of His Reign

> Say, is my kingdom lost?
> *Richard II*, Shakespeare

My sovereign. My love. I am what the truth
has eaten away to narrate this nightmare.
My face was still wet from mourning you—
that un-aimed arrow, flung east of the Jordan,
assuring you'd precede me into death's silted

shadow—when indelible hoofbeats of Jehu's
cavalry cut a swath through the vineyards
I gave you. In raiment and finery, face painted
in final radiance, I greeted him from our palace
window, tossed an insult that arrogant pretender's

way—words crass, bitter enough to make you proud.
But at his command I was thrown aloft by some
betraying eunuch's fist, like silk unspooled
into that burning blue air, the chorus of hounds
so perfect in hunger I could already see their teeth

bruised red, long before they reached our walls.
For uncountable moments I was so suspended
in light I almost wasn't falling. Almost thought
I wouldn't end like a Phoenician galley, in flames
on an ocean in which we were both suddenly thrashing.

Memorial Day Eve

With night fallen, I watch from my front step
the corner streetlight that seems to hover, illuming

nothing but a few passing cars and the neighbor
across the street who descends her driveway

to walk her dog. The American flag
silhouettes the blank green stucco wall

of her newly painted house. She fades down
a lane immersed in the amber halos of other

streetlights. Some recess of my mind
considers for a moment what women

who live alone do with their money
or their bodies, believe interior decorators

design for them décors of classical solitude.
A Pacific breeze rustles the night-dark

nimbus of camphor trees as she returns
upstreet, her ungainly shadow laboring up

her driveway. The sound of her door,
as it shuts, impels with it the utterance

of her last footstep, and the snap of the flag
still waiting to be folded at nightfall.

Blue Notes for Fireball Whiskey & Ginger Ale

I lost my audience at Northern Lights Lounge
when my solo sax got sloppy. Guess
I failed to fade my notes in fortissimo range.
Some ass in the Friday night crowd swore
I was washed-up, shouted for me to go back
to my day job—a shop rat turning bolts
at GM. The owner shook his head in dim
accord, a dirty change-up when he refused
to pay me for the gig. Hitting the street to find

my ride, a black cat didn't want to cross
my path, not even offer the mercy of its shadow,
the fellowship of burning yellow eyes.
When I got back to the Temple Hotel,
my woman warmed me with the whiskey
and tobacco burn of her tongue, all a man
like me ever needed in a bad time. When I told
her about Northern Lights, she glared at me
like a marked-down suit, said she couldn't

handle me losing one more job. She left Spam
frying on the stove and walked right on out,
her pace quickening with echoes, leaving
me like Eurydice in the underworld.
So I picked up my sax, opened the window
to the summer night, and hit a few overtones
in B-flat range, letting them weave into the screams
of Tiger fans cheering another win, my notes
and I, all the hunger an audience wants gone.

West Long Beach Littoral for Late April

There's a hotel without a name near Miramar
and Anaheim, where occupants drop
what possessions they own on dusty mattresses.
You didn't dwell long on whatever loss
brought you there, locked the door behind
you, and hit the twilight streets under a weak
moon rising in the soft impeachment of early
evening. At Rudy's Diner, you waited for a warm
meal dowsed in Tabasco, the heady acid
jolting a cough, a bite of hash browns chased
with bitter coffee. Bill paid, you passed a woman
at the entryway phone begging someone
in Spanish to please come home. Avoiding her eyes,
you paced west on Anaheim, stopped at Rosita's
Flowers, blossoms locked behind a thrown bolt.
Above, night birds fluttered from a window ledge
into wind rising shoreward that smelled of iron
and the sea. Reversing steps, you came to the railyard
at Cerritos Channel and paused, wondered
if there was more out there, knowing the answer
was a search for nothing promised, all thought
haloed under liquor store neon—an arrow aimed
inward like a one-way sign, nightfall bringing
all the sirens ever needed to sing your way home.

Waking Late for the Night Shift

Wind buffets her filmy bedroom window
from which a bowed figure is seen moving down
the street, going door to unanswered door, a street
named for flowers not found within miles of the city.

Looking skyward, she can't question metallic ash
soiling icy clouds above the refinery she works in,
nor freight cars at the edge of vision, laboring
slowly as if to give rail cops and switchmen the slip.

As her lover stirs, he can only offer her a weak,
drowsy kiss, so she moves downstairs to the kitchen,
her nude form shivering from a draft as she inhales
coffee steaming out of a cracked porcelain cup.

Leaving in work dungarees, a streetlight throws
her jagged shadow across the dark entryway
then down the front steps worn to anonymity,
snow falling softly as the door behind her.

The Soldier Willie McCausland Speaks of the Dancer
He Can't Take Home

Watching you twist inverted
toward the stage floor, my eyes
swear pole dancing comes
down to the physics of friction.

Baby, when you go on smoke
break inside that fenced
courtyard out back, I get lonely
as a pin pulled from a grenade.

As you reemerge inside, late
sunlight slips you through
a chorus of shadows. You pace
in a slow mercy toward my chair.

I lower the Drambuie from my lips
to let your breath blur with mine.
You, owner of pliant monikers,
how often you have saved men

from what they go home to, well before
you quit some a.m. hour, exit under
a bouncer's eye, your skin's glow dim,
the last light to go out in a ghost town.

Ranchero

It was supposed to happen only once.
Like calling some girl your steady, only
to have her call it off after your first date,
leaving with that icy huntress glare

my aunt Angelina bore when she knew
by my freshman year how yoked boys my age
were to emergent hungers. That first night
she'd gambled on what I hadn't yet known

of myself when she sealed her mouth to mine
and shoved me back against her '71 Ranchero
under ambient light of the 7-Eleven parking lot
where I worked, my boss still cleaning up

inside. Her hard whisper breathed through
a sneer, Not a goddamned word about this
to a soul, kid; it won't happen again; this woman
who'd never meet my eyes in the presence

of family, just her hand gently, safely,
on the shoulder of her favorite nephew
at gatherings after church, her print dress bright
as sails off Marina Del Ray, lipstick as dark

as the muscatel only she among the family
drank, my silence sworn for that woman
who, over years, was going to be that exposed,
that soft, and that impossible to wound.

What Sings Through Hostel Walls on Carondelet
for Father Jude LeBlanc

...the huge
Loose emptiness of light
Wheeling through everything.
Ted Hughes, "The Bird"

Nightlong, two pints of sherry, a couple's
past is resurrected in high-pitched laughter,
hurled about their room from a buckled sofa.
Through the papery wall that divides

our rooms it sounds like life was a narrow
escape back then—tangled or trapped in one grift
after another, days shortchanged and merciless.
Their voices finally simmer at 6 a.m. Day climbs

into gaunt shadows. The man leaves to peddle
street scams, passes our day manager whose eyes
are dark as Chekov winters, to head outside
to his '74 Pinto, its hulk a monument to rust.

The woman, just before noon, as is her habit,
will walk downtown, pass buildings that climb
against the weight of their Bourbon Street shadows
to sell herself amid secrets traded in the dusty light.

The fleeing hours and falling sun will bring them home
once more, stinking of everything the broken
streets offer—nothing that can ever be explained,
eluding the visible flaws in their lives.

My window's open to breezes off the riverfront. Soon
I'll hear them defeat the past with laughter again.
I won't stop listening, even with moths gathering
at my bedlamp with their numberless paper wings.

This Far North of Mojave
    for Joe Millar

Eyes tranced and bloodshot from hours on the road,
I pull off Route 101 to overnight in Gilroy. Everything
has found its place here. The odor of harvests grows
sere from drought. Water's reclaimed time and again,

like a weary forgiveness. Main Street has shrunk
to antique marts and thrift stores, the tithe of years.
Both coffee shops close on me before I reach their doors.
A bowling alley sign reads "Good Morning," no matter

the hour of day. Dogs thrive in the wider reaches
of the town. Reversing my route, I aim for the Chevron
with its food mart. A girl standing beside a blue
Camaro, Texas plates, smokes a bit too close

to the gas pumps. I watch her from the checkout
line, Slim Jims and a Mickey's 40-ounce malt
cold in my fist. Charley Pride, from the cashier's
radio, laments letters he'll never write home.

Now, every shadow retreats. At the Motel 6, I settle
behind double locks in a room around back, walls
stunned with yellow paint. I consider that young lady
back at the Chevron, the soft perfection of her slender

form inhaling tobacco burn like a backdraft, her hair
lifted into sunlight by a ribbon scarlet as regret.
In the all-night distance, the howl of passing trucks
is just far enough off to be a whisper in another room.

Desert Lover

Because want never takes a day off, the Nogales
hooker undulates with the sinews of a puma,
leaves her scent on every surface of you this morning.
After, out of words to praise her flesh, you simply
say how you love the desert she comes from.

All the while, she stared through a gap in the motel
curtain, said the desert's a dead planet to her,
but later lets you know how the wail of the Union Pacific
dissolves in the wash of distance. It's there forever,
she said, like the blue piano in A *Streetcar Named Desire*.

You think of your days patrolling the tar sands
of Tule Valley, how you were once a lean ranger
tracking feral horses, the many ranchers you called liars
for swearing the beasts were theirs—runaway or stolen,
how even then you waited for a world to come to you,
the desert beholden of your virile youth and Federal
badge, a pension guaranteed at the end of it all.

Now you watch the hooker at the bathroom mirror.
The near-reflexive way she dresses her paid-for
flesh. How her shoulders hold up those silk
straps as she paints the drugstore Revlon on lips
that swallowed you, the eye shadow she brushes on
for those eyes that took you all the way to silence.

Harbor Town Monograph

I.

I catch sight of a stray branch of rosebush
wilding through our ferns like a hand
under a green silk skirt. I ought to pull

it back, lattice it to the mother plant,
ensure its obedience upward into blossom.
But I can't help watching it lengthen along

its aberrant path. If I sit and wait till the sun
breaches maritime fog, a leaf-shadow
might skim the backs of my uneasy hands.

II.

From my front steps, the day is vapor trails
that lose altitude in distending signatures
that reflect off ice in my Sloe Gin glass.
A breeze swells a white curtain
in and out of a neighbor's window, the room
unlit behind it. The faint chime of an ice cream
truck fallows at the far end of an unseen
street, an altar bell in a dream. House
sparrows brush past, gray-brown chaff
that sieves the corner of vision, trilling
all they know in the space between us.

III.

The waterfront sky wanes to an ashen face.
It's gritty as homebrew dregs that stare
back from this chipped wine glass. Dark

seabirds spear overhead—tandem thieves
sliding east on a breeze of thin resolve.

Under the eaves, a farthing's worth of unfallen
sparrows are nesting in a biblical apparition.

A woman was mine here once, I think...
If so, it could've been her that slipped
the extra house key under my wiper blade.

Streetlights kindle their sodium vapor, one
by one, amber nets hauling darkness ashore.

Postcard Unsent

A Union Pacific diesel heaves the desert
night over the shoulders of its railcars.

The sallow moon threads its beam
through the spiked ribs of mesquite.

In a corner of Love's Travel Stop,
a trucker reads a letter in the moth-torn

halo of a streetlamp. Late tonight,
he'll stare his phone into never ringing.

The hand of a woman falling asleep
in the Motel 6, will drop a folded map

on the nightstand, the small towns
along the torn creases touching.

Eloy, Arizona

Late Trains at Landstuhl

Suspended in darkness, red signals
bookend the station. Couplings
groan like submarine hulls. Through
underground air lit with weak florescence,
passengers hurry between platforms.

On a bench recessed in shadow, a vagrant
pulls a coat around him. Rats, lean
as new moons, shuffle past, ignorant
of the man for whom sleep is mercy.

In anger over missing his train,
an accountant, wearied of the world's
numbers, grips a briefcase so tight
the blood disappears from his fist.

A woman, exiting the station, merges
with convergent streetlight halos
that double her shadow against a station
window. Castoff tickets wreathe
the pavement with spent travel.

Good Woman Gone

Morning is a motel's borrowed bed,
the hour edging forward into a day
layered with gray overcast, like a secret.
On my back, arms arched overhead,
my hands brush the headboard's wrought
iron, morning cold, a Bourbon Street
balcony summoned out of yesteryear.

A groundskeeper sweeps the parking lot,
slides the broom over the space her car
had been, as if to second her exit. Pausing
to wipe his brow, he pushes into the dustpan
the desiccate rasp of magnolia leaves, spent
cigarettes—their cooled crush of deserted ash.

Not yet 8:00 a.m. and I stretch myself
to her side of the bed, smoothing out
the imprint of her body on the sheets,
the warm depth gone out of them.

Gulls mount a sky beyond sight. A voice
on the alarm clock breaks open in mid-sentence,
warning of traffic down some road vital
to anyone but me. Next door, a maid bangs
about, her cell phone ringing a hymn in Spanish.

Idling in my vision, I think those are lilacs
she left behind, like frail blossoms of her voice.
In days ahead they will lose their scent,
their memory. Their secrets.

Till Quitting Time

Tobi Alfier

Jeff and Owen, till quitting time and beyond...

Amuse-Bouches

We are like roasted figs—
a little salt and pepper,
rosemary, olive oil,
whole milk ricotta.
Split wide and sinless.
***

"Grandpa, why is she laughing?"
"Well son, because she's happy"

"Grandpa, why is she crying?"
"Well son, because she's happy"
***

Needles and sunflowers.
One pierces my finger,
one pierces my heart.
A drop of blood burned
white on the table.
A glass of water
too still to keep life.
***

Winter angel—wings cracked,
grounded by ice, prisoner
of winter. Flat light, winter
light, quiet of winter.
Broken stone, heart of stone.
broken angel, quiet of heart.
***

Split wide and sinless,
a laugh and a cry.
Drop of blood burned
white on the table,
broken angel, quiet of heart,
Till quitting time...

Plum Trees and Women Next to the Applejack Tavern

Mottled gray, colors
marbled as if they've
been shirking in the
cellar for seasons,

and not breathing in
the scent of spring from
their hammock held by
firm, sunlit branches.

They hide a secret.
A vibrant ruby
secret. Sweet. Sexy.
And that is Emma.

Ripe and redheaded
Emma. So street smart,
she can order beer
in five languages,

but crumbles after
basic math. She will
make you want to cry
"Uncle" and marry

her at the same time.
She is your desire.
As long as she calls
you "honey" and not

some other guy's name
she'll be your passion,
your reason and your
nightmare—the woman

of all your wild nights.
Her hair the color
of poppies in spring,
she's been around some,

but you could care less.
Emma. Feed her plums.
Return her to spring.
Retreat there yourself.

Cape Split
    Cape Split is quite literally the "end of the world"
Google quote

      I

Pain is like the prenup you forgot to get,
it takes all the sweetness, leaves you
with the pawn tickets. You will never
be able to buy back an unfurled forehead,
true smile and the grace of comfort.

      II

So you sit in the bar, listen to complaints
of other people's unwanted houseguests,
drink just enough. One more winter
outlives its welcome as you as you lick
your cold lips, search for a warm face.

      III

The weather is ice over shade,
you need an elbow to pity you home.
This is not the first time. The tide is out,
you are resting on mud, you need a pilot,
who knows your analogies are weak

and your pride is mighty. Like a ship a-sail
with no engine, you pray for wind to lead you
past the soft swell of young lovers, to the breakwater
of hearth, to tea and the quiet compass of a stranger's
voice bidding you safe travels, small hurts.

Far West Texas
   for Lisa and Larry D. Thomas

A roan in a group of chestnuts—
solitary, as still as the sun that falls
on its back, shy as wandering
mule deer. Hummingbirds rev
wings, dip into sugar, buzz
in delicate arcs.

Sun and birds mark the odd damp cut
of river, surprise gash in the brown.
At first blush desolate, it teems
with wildflowers and wildness created
under turning skies.

Satellites and stars etch the blackness
at night, the way cloud-shadows punctuate
hills. Between them, pump-jacks and phone
lines—circuit board across the wide vast.
We stand, fragments against the infinite,
suspended in failing light.

The Angry Goddess of East-Coast Weather
for Jeffrey

Ice storm on the weather map,
a peculiar shade of white-pink
like porcelain angels, sugar dots,
and innocent intentions.

Not like the adolescent rebellion,
black eyeliner and destruction,
that causes you to stop cleaning
basement dust off the good china,

chip ice off your parents' front steps, wait
for the coming attack. My weathercaster
is miles from you, dressed for the tropics,
bare arms and loose hair—graceful hands

arcing the flow of storm. A northeast advance
of blush drapes over the rain-greens,
all moving in your direction.
I wish she were a liar.

She cautions that your Christmas
will be glacial, new snow clean
as confession, three times deadlier
than belief beyond doubt.

I am frightened for your numb hands,
cold feet, and the good Samaritan
in you, taking care of everyone else.
Jacket and coin mean the same to you,

and dangerous kindness will find you wanting.
Don't let that happen. When the power goes out,
and all is quiet as death, remember me,
after the solstice, face to the sun, waiting.

The Astronomer Measures the Distance to Living

He has always been able to measure intention.
He knows the waitress will pocket her tip,

the bartender will short half an ounce
on ten drinks, get plastered before

going home to lonely, but the girl?
To measure her is to begin to lose her,

and he cannot bear to fathom that.
He watched his daddy watch his mother

die, there was no measure for the sorrow.
The rows upon rows of yellow and gold poppies

and pills for pain, for pain, for more pain—
he cannot be that man. Medicine

and reading glasses on the counter,
her favorite book pockmarked with sorrow.

He never learned to measure that ability,
or desire, in himself—to say goodbye

and bless the broken angel,
to measure time not in loss, but in gain.

Back in His Arms Again

She loves quiet Sunday afternoons. She can feel herself sink into sleep in the comfort of the big green chair, familiar music that makes her feel like kissing playing on the radio on the window ledge. The occasional ping of her lover's computer and phone tells her someone is awake. Her lover reads by the light of the window, the gentle breeze brushing shadows from the camphor tree and climbing rose across his concentrating brow. He stops to answer his phone or stretch, or change the music, then goes back to his book. Sixty pages a day, that's his goal. Her goal is a dream of anything lovely—a waltz in the kitchen, fresh peaches on the porch, the tightness of his arms around her as he kisses her neck. Always a rosé from the South of France, though they don't drink rosé and have never been, their plans including other destinations but never France. She'd like to picnic on the bed with him, both wrapped only in the sheets. She'd like to wear a hat decorated with broad ribbons. She'd like to change her dream to hear the morning waking of the shore, the widening sound of tides as wind pours whispers through their open window like a sigh. Like her sigh, as she opens her eyes. Dance with me.

The Tall One

Has never been good enough,
never been pretty enough.
Children. Grandchildren. Never
enough. Never good enough.
She was "the tall one," the apple
of disappointment in a golden family.

She plays the fiddle as if Carnegie Hall
and Nashville refused borders. Tuxedoed
men in costly loafers and cashmere socks
keep time with the bearded and camo'd,
those somewhat left of the law on Wall Street,
Main Street, broken and flush—she weds them all,
and it means nothing special.

She knits a prayer shawl for a wayward fragment
of family heart. Blue the color of icy silence
and lost love. Fluttered edges and kind intentions
pray desperate wishes with each stitch.
When full enough to bandage years of venom
and scar, when the tears have dried like peeled paint
on the faded sills of unlived lives she will stop—
gift her plea for mercy and reconciliation.
For grace enough to humble any stoic heart.
She is a good and kind woman.
She is the tall one. Never enough.

Papa and the Glow of Mariachi

Papa's friend Uncle Tito always wore
a tweed jacket with suede elbow patches.
No matter the weather, that was his signature.

Good also for sitting at the wooden table,
elbows rested on the highly polished surface,
fake-burnt and oddly indented around the edges.

Drinking free tequila and juice, they discussed
their set, and took a moment of quiet before
singing—face to face, guitars with deep rosewood

bodies like sideways cellos. Like women.
They sparred through the dining rooms, talked
to patrons, refused all tips, stayed out of the bar.

Their sets always ended at a table in a side corner.
The gilt frame of an old mirror blessed by prisms
off a chandelier beamed the dampness of their

satisfaction, the way a gibbous moon tries
to light new lovers on an overpass to forever,
a pale melon tint silently mapping their way.

Our Town

The streets...
rusted cars
and vacant buildings
blighted,
as though rubbled
by hurricanes and war.
No mail is delivered here.
A cat prowls for food
in the cracks of sidewalks
and the dirt, empty
around tired trees.
A defeated factory,
a school, so broken
squatters don't bother
it with trespass.
Ancient air conditioning
units sag like impotence,
only the glare of sun
across half-broken windows
liked cracked teeth
throws beauty.
Turn off the radio,
bow your head with respect.
This lawless place,
genderless in age,
was your parents'
town once. They've
kept a few black & whites
to remember, scalloped
around the edges,
1964 crouching
low in each corner.

On the Perimeter of the Packard Plant
     Corner of Frederick & Bellevue, Detroit, Michigan

Cellblock, tenement, Dresden,
the color of dead December sky.

Not one of a thousand panes intact.
Some shattered in by throwing arms and dares,

some crushed among the rubble
by boredom, distrust, defeat.

Cement, brick, the odd mallet made in Japan.
This is a funeral with no wake,

no drunken dirges of hope, just drunks.
Just graffiti. Half a boat not shaped

enough for shelter or pleasure.
This blank-eyed stare of a city defines

the word gray as ugly. Even a kiss of snow
offers no redemption for rust.

Once the Dues Are Paid

He worked in the mill.
Until he didn't.
Now he works the chair,
inside the door, at the Alamo Bar.
It slouches in all the right spots
for his aching, defeated frame.

Light streaks in through the glass,
crosses his toes, lays a track
on the black and white tile.
A thin strip of sun shines
a stripe on the counter, just where
he reaches to pick up his drinks.

Beer in the morning. Boilermakers
at lunch. Whiskey straight, by evening.
He's got coins for the jukebox, smiles
for the waitress, creaks and mutters
for everyone else. Booze and small
kindnesses. Till quitting time.

Tune-up

He loves in the way the used-to-be green
Chevy advances up and over

the hill—engine churning its last leg
rumble. Invisible until cresting into view,

a little rust added for wry charm, baggage
of old receipts and papers in the back.

He ignites. Like the crack of a ground ball
charging past the reach of a desperate glove,

a strike of heat lightning in a dry field.
Explosive. Immediate. Unstoppable.

She loves in the way an orchestra tunes up.
Tentative, yet deliberate, playing the scales

of possibility while ensuring fine melody
and perfect pitch. Strong hands comfort

the most fickle of strings, of reeds with histories
back to time's beginning. A countenance

of concentration. Quiet as she gains
confidence, she will bring you memories

with lush harmony. Hers is a slow smolder.
To watch them both is to learn the way ice melts

in a glass, tempering heat, cooling the tongue.
You sit on the porch of observation,

watch the streetlights come on, learn how
carburetors make music. A question is answered.

In Flight

Milky sky and my tired eyes
conceal Lake Michigan, 30,000 feet
below, making her presence known.
Both on maps, and with the violence
of a policeman shaking a sleeping drunk,
this is no smooth sky.

Flying into the sunrise is like standing
on lava. The blackened beach of night
streaked with fire, a long-haired exotic
woman, hair cascading down brilliantly
colored fabric. You watch from a distance,
cannot describe this quietly active sky.

And then the thunder. Explosive,
a jealous lover, a raging canopy.
Every emotion controlled and out of control
with perfect timing. The moon cringes.
The sky plays chess.

Small Portraits

Carol Berg

First Self-Portrait

and so it was that the plants animated her   she peeled

white birch bark and formed her back   she wove the bindweeds

into her hair pink and tight   wove and wove

she swallowed the rhizome of the iris and so it was

her iris unfurled and she planted roots and tubers inside her

-self urging them to stretch into clavicles and blades and so it was

she molded the green quince into her heart

and foresaw that he would eat of it

Self-Portrait as Farmer's Market

I am the sweetest thing
you will ever put in your mouth
I am orange cherry tomatoes
I am candy-colored beets
I am stalks and stalks
of red yellow yellow red
gladioli   I am poesy of zinnias
and other wildflowers
I am tassel and kernel
of buttery corn on the cob
I am yellow plum tomatoes
I am an arm-length English
cucumber I am ready
to bruise peaches I am homemade
poppy seed bagels I am local goldenrod
honey oozing in a jar

Self-Portrait as Wife as House as Housewife

The gold chain wrapped around
your throat menaces me.
The sky is in the basement with
empty beer bottles and discarded baby
seats. You think mice have invaded
but really they're clouds making all that mess
clouds that risk their throats for the steel you've
laid bare. You come in with your tools
and bring me down down the stairs
again to show me. The goats are tied up here
bleating. I want their solace I want
their sturdy hooves. The dryer turns
its unconventional rotation into a study
of wheels of cogs of squeals. I squeeze
the washcloths and soap refuses
to come out to release itself to vacate.
I wish for the vacancies of garages
of cupboards holding the last of the Halloween
candy bars. I try to refuse the bleach you
offer try to refuse your stares.
Your leash singing on the hook.

Self-Portrait as Dangerous When Down

Should I go running today? Should I
climb trees? When should I shower

and how much time should I spend on
the computer? How much time should I spend on

my son? Keep trying to teach him how to tie
his shoelaces but I get so impatient.

It doesn't get done.
I tell him the laces are too long.

But I am baking the bread today mixing yeast
with warm loving water adding sugar and salt

for the yeast to feed on change into bubbles
like laughter under water and then the King

Arthur's Flour, no, wait it's the on-sale crappy
flour. Three teaspoons equal one capitalized

tablespoon since I lost our only silver
measuring spoon. Threw it away, probably, in the trash,

mixed in with beet skins and eggshells.
There is a wire fallen down onto our mailbox

an electrical mistake. If only our bills
would catch on fire sizzle and snap into something

I can't possibly send back. Consider all downed wires
to be energized the National Grid website says and oh if only I were

considered as dangerous when I was down.

Self-Portrait as Book of Self-Portraits

I taste of words.
In my lower back, I am butter and crescent
shaped. My heart is a mezzaluna,
half moon, that cuts and chews.
I walk down my spine,
trying to understand
myself. I am preacher and Marie
Antoinette. In the elevator, we receive
vertigo. I look around for Shakespeare's
delicate eyes. He would play my disguise:
a boy with so many mouths like nibbling
goldfish and a string of Christmas
lights. And then suddenly we descend. The skulls
and bones perfectly laid out. Even here, I am water
dripping. I am the evidence we carry out.
I am muscle, venom. Now I am
everything you have read in your hands.

The Apple Speaks

When you choose me
think of spring blossoms

small phoebes on a twig
with their tails

twitching, readying
for the chase of mayfly

or mosquito. Think
of the unfurl and the smell

of pink, the bark of childhood trees.
When you hold me

in your hand I am
the squeezable breast

the promise of a heart
you can break apart and eat

then flick away the seeds.
No rancor, no pleas.

Palette of red,
how I blend with yellow

into orange, a sunset.
My skin spattered with stars.

A canvas of unnamed
constellations. And when you finally

bring me to your lips
remember

once I was part sky
once you were part forest.

Portrait With Yeast
      for Ruth Foley

For seven days she watches the metamorphosis
from champagne grapes to white froth.
She feels like she's in fourth grade again
lifting the glass jar from the terrarium and inhaling
moss and the dampness of a world she wanders
into and makes her own. Now here in her own home
within the walls she had scrubbed and painted sea-glass
green she sprinkles the yeast she had created herself
into glass bowls, adds flour, salt, cinnamon.
She pats the messy dough until it forms itself,
slips it into the greased pan. She sets
the timer and imagines the moment when she will cut
into the still warm bread, butter it, and watch as her
husband wordlessly brings so much of her into his mouth.

Self-Portrait as Waterworld

I am your amusement ride.
I am tattoos and belly bolts.
You will stand in a solitary line.
There is a funhouse.
I will spurt for you. I will twirl.
I will blister the bottoms
of your feet. There will be
screams and the sounds
of propulsion. My running
water will sort your bones
by size. There is a luminescent light
a white like something held
inside the body, teeth or bone.
The signs, the maps. You are here.
Still. Someone always disappears.

Self-Portrait as Insomnia

I rose into the moonlight
that white flock of tiny engines
muffled motorcycles revving many hearts
beating and all of them were mine
and we came to the mountains where your sister
died all rock and boulder and Indian paintbrushes
flaming the night red and yellow eyes and the panther
moon pacing licking its black fur and all I can do is turn
over into four o'clock four o'clock four o'clock

Self-Portrait as Dragonfly

Attired in black and white this year, I wear
the formal evening all season long. Last year

I wore a modern metallic so blue it hurt
the sky's eye. He leads me around by my

neck, holding my lacy clasp. How his
cummerbund cinches my back.

My wings made out of translucent glass
stitched together like some cathedral window.

My wings rotate and move forward.
With each stoke I use the unsteady air studded

with the energy of a diamond's burn. When I rest,

my wings mold together above my back.
No other insect wears such a darkness in their wings.

Self-Portrait as Beet

My cycle of redness has begun.
Even in your winter white I boil red.

Your napkins your fingertips will dye
red. There will be the taste of graduation

carnations. In your hands my skin
slips. You toss away my greens

Yet still I believe. I believe in compost.
I believe in reincarnation.

I depend upon the blessings of kosher salt.
The sacrificial goat cheese avoids me.

The olive oil speaks its ornate
language of trees to itself.

Still, even I can look innocent
while bleeding on your white plate.

Self-Portrait as a Glass of Chardonnay

In your fragile kitchen,
do you hear my clang and feel my stare?

There will be a flight
of roaming heartbeats

and a drumming at five
in the morning. Commit yourself
to the taste of guilt.
I exude the scent
of satin sheets, of a green
appetite. Think of your
neighbor's dismay and close
your eyes. Twirl and think torque,
think split. Unfit.
Between thumb and fore-
finger, you hold my stem precariously.

Self-Portrait as Bumblebee Knocked Between Your Bare Thighs

I heavy with sun
flower pollen feel
the slow division between
summer and fall, light
and death attenuate the silk
web thread ready to snap
and whip my wing-map
into snips and hear
the hive-thought thrumming
urgent surge me forward amid
all the children's mothers steering their
run-impoverished energies into cars
and I dodge the wind raindrops
crows but you two leggedly
for an impossible moment net me.

Self-Portrait as Seer

There is a shape to my darkness to my lost
bones. I chew the enamel from my chipping
teeth, chew on my misfiring synapses.
Inside my head I sit in all the empty
pews. Light up all my orange candles
chanting in the language of fragments.
Inside my head the flocking birds, the constant
veering wings. The unstoppable
vines spinning through my veins.
My mouth filling up with unspittable seeds.

Small Portrait
    after the painting of the same name by Kay Sage

For you I have finally peeled back
the skin-colored disguise from my face. Underneath,
the iron gate. The subtle hinges. I know you
think there is a lock. See the scaffolding that curves?
It protects the thin metal pilings crosshatched. All held
up by the buckling cinderblocks sometimes mistaken
for my mechanized smile. The "apparent" buckling—
but see the engineering feats I am constructing
underneath. Panta rhei: All things
in flux. Zigzag bronze plates for cerebral hemi-
spheres. No I will not explain the uses of my russet
hair. Just know that when you touch my cheek
the skin the bones the flush feel real.

Reverse Commute

Ana Maria Caballero

Timing

Sunday taxi from the airport
        To the house

An hour passed amongst
        Children

Things set down in a place
        Reserved

Electric clouds to yoga
        The intentioned drive

A practice repeated endeavored
        Offered
/Over

The sushi chef mentions the score because
        I am there

Tomorrow he will prepare
        My broth

The sky drizzles headlights flaunt
        The rain
/Again

There are no brief moments that pass
        Us by

The Public

Born of the first stone, I am witch:
Spellbound by small elements,
snails in the throat, birds on the lip.

There is a hiding behind the trunk
of a dead tree, a memory
of morning, a reckoning.

There are no men, no children.
No women with soft worries.
No confidences or shared will.

But when I blow the lonesome wind,
the wooded land breathes in.
Together we become the ancient word,

a god released.

Limbs

The wind exists to blow the pages
of the book I read.

My book exists to be read by me
resting on its wind.

Its pages are   to be the book
blown by the wind that blows
my book.

So I,
I am the book and its shuffling pages,

                        that become wind
                        through the sound of bending,

                        that return the book to its life on paper
                        and rouse the body to its life on limb.

Said and Done

I fear my capacity to guide
Mistake toward fulfillment

At times, I blame:

> The flurry of misprint,
> of crisis to unscramble;
>
> The renewed promise
> of classic self-improvement;
>
> The flat-water buoyancy
> of fresh peace.

Other times, I blame:

> This devotion
> to words and their construction—
>
> How they unsay as they say—
> How they commit to purpose as thought—
> How they slay aim through speech—
> How they make me prove and reprove this power—
>
>
> This lack.

Tragedy at Sushi Siam

Today I read about poetic time and poetic space,
about how allegories are imagined and metrics not.

I read about real efforts to compose,
allusions, footnotes, toolsheds as help.

I read all this believing in it,
not knowing that tonight you would be where I was,

and I would need to come home to think about you
in recent time, in recent space.

Gradual Rot

Rot is a gradual process. It begins while the fruit is ripe and dangling from the tree. Once it falls, the process is in full, and the fruit must be thrown away or eaten quickly.

I have picked mangoes off the ground of warm places because they taste good when they are just about bad. They are also delicious before they become ripe. Mangoes are an exception.

But, this is not about exceptions. This is about the gradual process of rot, even while clinging to a tree. Even while young and pleasant, with clean clothes and comfortable heels. Being mindful of the ground does not mean being ready for the fall.

Casualty

Casually we harden:

sky-wide interactions that grow   condensed
reduced as
         rain.

I classify your hands,
       keep mine filed
       inside the loose jackets
       we once wore.

       They hang—
       each
          on its own.

There is mention of the hardening,
a sharing of its separate ways.

But we keep it soft
in the mellow-minded amicable   banter

of our
     love.

A *Notion of Marriage*

Because I am a poet,
I read about things like the center of skin.
About warm bodies coming together in the dark,
and how it can be the meaning of life
when someone gets it right.

And I know I should write about things
like a moving chest and a naked back.
About the coming together of life in the dark,
about our common desire
and the verbs that it took.

And it should be universal,
but personal.
My moving chest, your naked back.
The notion of marriage,
of children, of daily love.
Shrinking rooms
beneath the surface
of different meaning words.

But I don't see the dark jaw
in the night,
or the soft center of touch spring alive.
There is effort and a plan.
There is marriage,
a shrinking room,
daily love,
and a baby that eats time.

We do not say flesh when we mean sex.
We say it's about right.
And, it would be nice.
We confirm how long it's been
before we ask the other to get up
and make our narrow bedroom
dark.

Lunchtime

When I don't go out to talk lunch talk
I stay home and we eat lunch

We don't talk but we make delicious food noise

You launch the silver; I scoop it up—
just to watch your face hear it crash

I let you play with fruits that stain—

A wet bill, a torn book, a cracked phone—
proof in my hand that your new body leaves a mark

I offer you the tiny shoe you love to chew

Together we prepare
for a time when things might not be good

Baby

You are
A long time
Coming

Now
All time is
Your time

My time is
Yours since
Before

But your
Time is
Not mine

It is yours
I get to
Watch it

Feel how
You are not
In me

But you were
There you
Grew

Into a paw
Of blood
And time

It felt good
To share
To receive

Now I live
To give
You time

Babies on Planes

When I am on a plane
and I hear a baby cry,
I think: cry, cry, cry.

Cry slower and louder.
Cry longer.

Cry while your mother walks you around;
may the entire plane hear you cry.

Stop crying, whimper softly,
make us think you might be done,
        then bawl.

When the flight attendant offers help that is not help—
shriek. Howl the flight attendant away.

Make your mother give up,
display her shabby grin
and descend into her seat.

Cry right into the immigration line, right into my ear.

Cry right into the wait for bags
that are not there and do not come and still
they do not come.

Screech on the airport curb;
howl inside your car.

When you are gone, keep the ringing faint,
but keep it real, keep it long.

Scream baby, baby.

Rack up my airplane baby miles
for the airplane baby day
when my baby decides to cry.

Paco

Last night, I heard Paco de Lucía play the guitar
in a theater cut out of a dry rock in the South of Spain.

My father could not go because he fell
and hit his head
and has been in bed for fifteen days
and it could be longer.

My brothers are not here and do not know.

So I went with my mother
to see men with faces that look like the first face,

the face of the Gypsy and the Jew,
the Arab sage and the hanging Christ.
Hair around the eyes,
a focusing view of enemy foot
through rising desert sand.

El Farru, the great flamenco dancer,
danced in the middle of the music men
and lost a dancing heel
in the middle of the song.

The dead heel lay dumb
like a bitten fig
while El Farru beat his sounding heel down.

Then he bowed
and held up his mute heel to make our hands applaud.

De Lucía. His nephew-apprentice to the left.
The singers with no voice, dry rock slicing their throats.
The bass that seized a place and played a role.
The flamenco hair whipping Farru's face
like a despot rider his despot horse.

I filmed it all to show my father.
But the clip will deepen
the slip of the heel and the dry rock
against the head.

So I keep it for my mother
for when she'll need her music men.

Yellow Tomatoes

I once thought I could know anything

The death knowledge of the Buddha
The clarifying call of Gabriel
Former lives and abetting suns
That enthrall worlds more able than mine

I too never doubted my time supply
To be the daughter to the dying father
Who buries without the blow of love regret

But my father is dying an excessive death
With a wounded body
That aligns rare moments of life
To the faint efforts of his mind

And I do

I offer my happy baby's dance
Ask about our mayor and the bad president
So together
We can wave our related heads with a laugh

I bring home the foods he likes to eat
Chocolate sugar-free
A bag of sweet yellow tomatoes
That falls when his good hand forgets to grab

And when he insists on phoning my mother
Makes a promise that he won't speak drink
I dial

I do I dance

Far from the Buddha knowledge of the giving death
Deaf to the recurring chant of Gabriel
Books by my bed and worlds of grace
That I grasp
But lack the good hand with which to grab

Revisiting the Account of Daphne and Apollo

Jennifer Finstrom

Upon Revisiting the Account of Daphne and Apollo in
My Grandmother's Copy of Bulfinch's The Age of Fable

When I think of transformation, I don't only contemplate the
plight of Gregor Samsa, voiceless and changed on the wall of his
room. I think too of the *Metamorphoses* of Ovid, of Zeus and
Apollo, Io and Daphne, Europa on the back of the white bull.

In Greek mythology it is not safe to be a girl. I page through my
grandmother's copy of Thomas Bulfinch's *The Age of Fable*, read
about Daphne and how "many lovers sought her, but she
spurned them all," read how "Apollo loved her, and longed to
obtain her," and then—when I had always imagined her free
though transformed—read how Bulfinch writes of the tree's
gratitude for the god's regard.

I wrote a poem about Daphne once, saw the woman in the tree
growing toward the sun, in love at last with the pursuing heat.
Now I would revisit that poem and tell the reader that there are
clouds and storms, long cool nights when the tree stands alone
and quiet. I would write that the sun is only a part of the story.

Almost Sonnet Written While Considering Annotations
I've Made in an Old Copy of Euripides' Medea

"The mind of a queen is a thing to fear." -EURIPIDES, Medea

I still have the paperback copy of Medea
that I carried everywhere my sophomore
year of college. On the margins of an early
page, well before she vanishes in a chariot
drawn by dragons, before banishment,
before the gift of a poisoned robe
for her husband's new bride, I have written
in neat cursive that "magic set Medea apart"
and "she is both witch and queen." And later,
that "she understands what she does, even as
she does it." My cursive now is never
so precise, and I wonder where the girl who
wrote those words has gone. A woman sleeps
in my bed, and I have given her nothing.

Missing the Stars

Here in the city, I seldom
notice the stars. Tonight I rode
the elevator down thirteen
floors with my garbage and
surprised a feeble glimmer
above me by the alley dumpster.
In early December, the daylight
disappears by five. The fenced
lot across the way holds
rottweilers, thick jointed and
no longer young. They watch
my retreat with hostile, amiable
faces and snuffle rather than bark.
Back in the elevator, I think
of Orion, and how I would
see him in the winter months
when we lived in Milwaukee.
I waited tables first shift then,
and it would still be night
when I crept into the predawn
chill to warm up the car.
In that raw sky, Orion
seemed more than a blinded
huntsman, pitied by the gods.
I felt he was responsible
for the morning's activity of buses
swinging into their routes,
paperboys crunching over frosty
grass, the old man ambling
with his fat and ancient spaniel.
And I thought of the time
before everything was named,
when the sky was still empty
and anything could be placed
for safekeeping in its limitless
dark cupboards. Club and
lion's skin, belt and sword, even
a giant man leading his eternal
dog on a walk through the sky.

Ariadne

The white bull came
in my mother's time.
He circled the palace
like a steaming
wheel and would not
calm. This was
not Zeus, though my
mother believed otherwise.
She was a young
bride then and new
to the island and its
ways. The bull
was beautiful, pure
white and crowned
with horns. Things
that come from
the sea are meant
to return, my father
said. He pressed
for sacrifice. The sun-
warmed throat and heavy
head bowed to my
mother's lap. She kept
his blood shut tight.
Together they watched
the waves that pushed
him out. Violently.
Like a great shipwreck.

Naxos

I am outside myself
watching; I am inside
the dream.
I am watching
the ship grow small,
watching the man
mount the ship, watching
him point to the sea.

I am watching
the sea surround him
like a vast black
hand, like
a maelstrom mouth,
like the unshut eye
of an ominous god.

Daedalus

The men in the harbor
were awake to see
us go. They gripped
rope and sail,
shouted as we rose
in a rush of gulls.
Soon they were
nothing, and even Crete
fell away
like a blown map.

Between sea and
sky, a road
appeared, unspooling
like a thread
of fire. I saw
wheels and horses
made of light,
my son
greeting the man
who held the reins.

Prophetess

I stopped being a girl a long time ago. He first
whispered words of love to me when I was four,

a child in the splash of sunshine at my mother's
feet. I was six before I saw he was the sunshine,

eight before I knew he was a god. But the visions
came as soon as I could speak to tell of them,

pictures stabbing themselves like chopsticks,
daggers, the bloodied beaks of swans. The nerves

in my eyes burned pink and glaring as boiled
shrimp, and still I waited for him, hugging

my knees, nursing my mutant longing
for a man who wasn't a man. When I sleep,

the sun shoves the moon, forces her away over
night's hills. Nothing shines from her cold

temple, but in the darkest hour she whispers
to me of polar regions where the sun is dead,

where even his love can't find me.

Daphne and Apollo

This silver thread is the water
where he gave me up. He never
comes so close, but rolls his course,
covers the hills, this river, my rigid
self with gold. The land still knows
the touch of heaven. Daily I recall
the story, see again the fleeing girl,
the pursuing god, the flames
already running in their wake.

Other women wed with gods and live.
They bear strange fruit, are touched
but not consumed. My last morning
brought someone walking out of the sky.
He rippled down, held droplets on his flesh
of tiny light. He was clean with air.
And still, slow growing, I raise
my arms to heaven. And return
to him unhurried, leaf by leaf.

The Fates

Even the Fates must have been young
once, sisters moving in unison.
Three parts of the same being—
three pairs of arms to spin, measure,
and cut. Their hearts not cushions
but machines, following each other
like drumming footsteps, an army
on the march, steady and echoing.

Do they speak to each other as they
toil and wonder at the absurdity?
*Too long. Too short. What is
the point?* Or do they fail
to understand mortality and its torn

cocoon? The attics of their minds—
more hard drive than musty clutter—
hold an infinity of ticking clocks, and
their youth, if they had it, might
be found among the gears and shifts.
Or did they wake already old to find
the yarn twisting in their hands,
beginning its relentless unwinding?

Circe in the Upper Peninsula

This June, blocks of ice still float
in Lake Superior, the water temperature
not even reaching forty degrees.
The air is at eighty and climbing,
and swimmers brave the cold
to pose on ice floes in bikinis.

Before the ice melts, my father
sends me a picture from *The Mining
Journal*, a stark photo of a young
woman sitting on the beach, arms
wrapping her legs as she
regards the bobbing islands
that reach out past the ore dock.
He has sent the picture because
he thought I might like to write
a poem about the woman
contemplating the horizon as if
waiting for someone or something,
even if only for the ice to melt,
and I do want to write that poem

but can't help but think of another
poem I wrote in the late 1980s
when I went to school in Green Bay.
That earlier poem might have been
called "Circe in Northern Wisconsin"
or "Circe as a College Sophomore,"
but I called it "Circe's Lament"
because of the time I spent gazing
at another lake and trying to summon
a boy from its depths, from the rushing
of waves and wind in my ears.
And I remember, too, the blizzard
one spring, in May, when I didn't

know classes were canceled and ended up
moored to my waist in a drift, my path
through the snow the wake left
by a swimmer before she drowns.

And then, as now, I envy Circe,
living almost alone,
and I see her in the picture
of the woman on the beach,
and those blocks of ice that so
passively float might be the men
she has changed beyond returning,
diminishing with every coin
of light the sun spends,
waiting only for summer's
slow dissolve into the sea.

Hades, Hermes, and Persephone in Fullerton Hall

"Word Outleaps the World":
Readings and Dance, The Art Institute of Chicago

He looks the part: dark hair that's a little
long, taller than the other man who dances
the role of Hermes bringing her back
to the sunlit meadow. Though we in the audience
do not see the pale narcissi and other flowers,
it is easy to imagine them blooming on the bare
stage. In the same way, we imagine
the earth splitting open, consenting
to invite her into its numerous dark rooms.

Earlier in the performance, these same two
had been Hector and Achilles, struggling
together with the death between them, the dark
one left, at last, on the floor of the stage.
And I can't forget a moment that happened
before they became the Lord of the Underworld
and the Messenger of Olympus, when the woman
who was Persephone was just a dancer.
As he passed behind her, the man who would become
Hades reached out a familiar hand, unseen
by most of the audience, and pulled down
the woman's black lace top—where it had slid
up—to cover the revealed inch of skin.

Moments later, the three are navigating the long
winter road: dancing blizzard, dearth, and famine,
the death of seeds in the cold earth.
Some invisible mineral binds them to each other.
In this way she is called back each year,
whether she has learned to love him or not.

Some Poems Are Spells

If someone takes you and puts you
in a poem, of course it isn't really you,
just as a doll stuck full of pins late at night
isn't really the boy in the girl's mind.
But just the same, if someone takes
a you that isn't you and puts you
in a world that isn't real, something
still happens. It might be more accurate
to say that a poem creates myth and
that every poem writes its own labyrinth,
is its own hidden minotaur, and you must
decide if you are Theseus or Ariadne,
Daedalus or Icarus. You must decide
if, reaching the poem's heart, you
will try to kill it or live in it.

Minotaur

If seen in uncertain light, he
is little more than a powerful
man, a figure sheathed in muscle,
the curving horns that crown
him lost in shadow. He could
be stone, a statue, alert
for the girl's light footfall,
her breathless whisper. When he
stands, his horns strike sparks.
The ring in his nose, the width
of a woman's palm, could lead
him when he was a bull child
but no longer. He knows
every step of the trap he lives
in, can shamble its blind turnings
as he sleeps and dreams, and
though he is neither prince
nor god, they will always
come, bringing gifts.
If Crete is a human body,
he knows he is not its head
or heart, not its soul or
aspirations. Rather, he is
the nightmare that haunts it,
the lust that drives it, the monster
that sets every man apart.

Almost Sonnet Written While Thinking about First Love,
Greek Mythology, and The Great Gatsby

What assumptions I made about love when
I was in high school came from Greek mythology
and *The Great Gatsby.* I feared that loving a man
would lead to some inevitable transformation
and looked at the trees I passed walking home
as if they had once been girls. I envied them
their solitary, twisted state and felt that my own
arms were too weak and yielding. I thought that
love led always to death and that whatever I wanted
would kill me and read often the passage near the end
where he had "paid a high price for living too long
with a single dream." Even last year, I said to a friend,
"He's my Daisy. I might die of this." But I didn't.

Bliss, Not Weight

Joanie Hieger Fritz Zosike

Amputees
December 4, 2011, New York City

A one-legged man sat in his wheel chair
Regarding a three-legged chair kneeling on the sidewalk
"What you need is some wheels, my friend,
Said the man with a knowing wink

But the chair wasn't having any of this
"What you need, sir, is some sensitivity!
You have no idea what I've been made to endure:
Pompous asses, fat asses, bony asses—all kinds of asses!"

The man considered this varnished diatribe and replied,
"I feel for you, my friend, but take courage
Whereas you've been set upon by being sat upon,
I've been put upon and blown apart by poverty and war"

The chair could not, however, be consoled
"My man, your kind never learns its lessons
You just plunder and splinter folks like me in rainforests
Then exile us to your infernal ass-populated cities"

The man was beginning to lose his good humor
"Now listen, you dried-out confabulation of sorry twigs,
I approached you with friendship and compassion
But now you're starting to work my last nerve"

"You watch your supercilious trap," the bitter chair spat,
"I lost my home, my leg and my moms; Got no job, yo—
No woman, no insurance—could you just help me out?"
The three-legged chair leaned pitifully on the concrete

But by now the one-legged man was disgusted
And he rolled away softly whistling "Alouette"
While the chair was left to ponder its gnarly fate
For the rest of its wooden-headed days

Day After Labored Day...A Riff on an Old Flame
September 7, 2014, New York City
                    for Craig

Thirteen years after, her fragrance
Intimately lingers in the atmosphere
The blight of a tart necrotic fever
Tugs the phantom tissue of vigor
Drags him deeply under pavement

She often calls him downtown
Beckoning with falcon talons
A statuesque solo figure primping
She ingratiates herself on oglers
Who pay homage to a silver calf

Come meet me at the SW corner
Near the NE entry where people gather
To blink at a circle of patriotic trees
Uniformed guards parrot their script
He asks, Whodunit, my mystery?

Tourists finger her pools, posing
With goofy smiles and hip-hop hands
As if it's Sunday in Coney Island
Burnt odor tantalizes his nostrils
Brittle follicles spit grit on his lips

Oblivious of her rebirth, she probes:
Do I still sizzle your trachea, baby?
Grip your spleen and wind your gut?
Sparkle gaily in your shivering liver?
Steal tracings of your sporadic sleep?

He dreams of birds, unnamed homeless
He walks through time-walls to activate
Service drones responding automatically
With blame, fire, riptide, torn diligence
A tide of flesh financed by war chests

What happened? She keeps demanding
Pebbles! he shouts. Crisp bones on roofs!
Furious spittle, so that zealots may deploy
Children as fancy high-wire dancers
Solemnly traversing a sinewy spine

2015–Colonial Drive
January 1, 2015, New Paltz, NY
for Susan

The gift gifting is not over.
Nor should it ever be.
Give from your heart always.
As if you are giving to yourself.
And do give to yourself
(my unsought advice to me).
The holidays reside then resolve
Like a great big O
(ya know what I mean).
 Never despair, be of good cheer.
The feelgood doesn't melt away yet
Hot tears of unintended witness stay

Enter we into the revolution
(for another year such as this last
cannot be tolerated,
ya know what I mean encore).
Once more on our sail around the sun.
We are so sew up the Tree of Life.
The finality of this year's end
(goodbye, good riddance except for
last year's blessings, count your own
as I do mine, and there were blessings)
Doesn't bolster the lie that at last
Everything will be better.

Everything will not be better.
Everything will be what it is,
What it shall be. We may think we're
The director but we are bit players in
A drama without direction; can't see
It's another mixed bag of fertilizer
smelling things up before the pleasure
Of the threshing. Will this be a

106

Hard cold year replete with fake
Smiles, bear hugs and oily slugs;
With annoyance but still buoyant

Notwithstanding, willfully we will
Do our best to understand—ah, hell!
LET US BEGIN!

Judith Malina (6-4-26 to 4-10-15)
April 10, 2015, Manchester, NJ

I keep my silence as I often do when life reminds me
We are ephemeral as the dew, we blow in the wind
As Judith would say: "I'm running a race with Death,
And I know Death will outrun me, but meanwhile, I'm
Still winning." Today, beloved heart, death has won

Or did s/he? Oh, Malach ha-mavis I fought with you
Before, after, during this sad day. I have lit my candle
White for purification in the face of the biggest thief
On earth. I defy you, Malach ha-mavis, to convince
Those of us on this plane, that our Judith is gone

She lives within us, through all she has taught us
Over the years, on the boards, under the influence
After the rainfall, inside utopia, outside of Paradise
Standing at the gates and railing, "I'm not allowed
To travel without a passport." Malina, my teacher

I will remember the warmth of your tiny hand in mine
I will remember your eyes flashing when we argued
Which we did too often for two who had such love
And deep respect for each other and for life. You so
Pure and resolute, I so filled with doubt and willful

The world has lost a great soul today; I've dreaded
This day since I met you, as one often does with
One's great loves. You were one of mine, and you
Leave behind, as great teachers do, the sweetest
Of scents to anoint us with enduring hope

The Nose's Tale Proprio
October 20, 2014, Van Nuys, CA

1.
She wakes with irritation at air filling her lungs.
Daylight tickles the back of her optic nerve with
Otherly, motherly, at times, brotherly tenderness
She resents day's rude intervention on her night

"I don't want to be this way, Daddy!" she cries out
To The Nose. "Always carping. I want to ripple into
Sudsy daybreak till it erupts as a bubble rhapsody
Crooning all day about life as bliss, not weight."

The Nose on the wall, no surprise, is silent
Noses don't talk. Nor do dead Daddies
She throws herself onto the bed with a passion
Longing, reaching past respectable boundaries

She tiptoes into Immutable, a land where few
Venture without fear; places a tentative foot in
Proceeds to the far side. She feels tactile arms
Embrace her. "I am always with you," he says

She quotes that line too often; no one knows
About the crumbs she tosses aground so as to
Retrace her steps back to a world without him
The one everyone agrees upon as real life

Oh? How can it be real with him gone? Yet
It smells real, has the same motley topography
Such is the mystery of absence, so weirdly
Present when a beloved slips into the abyss

To emerge as an eye, a nose, a blemish on a
Blameless wall, trumpeting the declaration
"I'm here." Peer beneath the surface at either
Side of the cleft. There's open space aplenty

To receive you with something bright and full
As the morning that she greets with irritation
Coating her lungs and toes, her nose is clogged
With detritus from a quagmire of rootlessness

2.
Cheekbones jut out from the curtain. No breeze
To check persuasive Slavic bone that protrudes
Outward to greet a Romanesque nose, tossing
Cloying comments from the perpendicular wall

She identifies the contours of his cheek, poised
Over his violin measuring noble phrases of Bach
Devoted Bloch and devilish Paganini on the roof
Cheekbones tilt up and down with bowing mirth

What goes with this partially featured face
Engine and brain do not appear intact yet
His essence crowds the room with rich sound
Soaring to the sunshiny corners; sizzling will

Wants to fill in the volume and mass of an
Orchestra that awaits, or predates his exit
Watching from the pit as a little girl I recall
How proud I felt as the string section played

3.
Santana winds whip down Santa Susana Canyon
Where the Chumash ancestors once walked softly
Summer is officially over; in blowoy Simi Valley
Ronald Reagan's Library flashes a showy grin

Simi is the fifth happiest city in the United States
There are few books in Reagan Memorial Library
There are barely any memories amidst the vapid
Grinning aisles; the winds blow dust and minds

I lie on the bed and listen to howling banshees
Blustering, blubbering, they seem to recollect
The Natives who once walked softly, who walk
No longer; still most everyone is happy in Simi

Stilled voices and silenced footfalls also inhabit
The Coachella Valley, where the Santa Ana winds
Lash the dirt and spread grey sand in gritty waves
Deserts are like dried-out seas that spawn tsunamis

Light and shadow illuminate the bedroom curtain
A shadow play of water lilies and desert roses fly
In eddies against a cold beige background, then a
Crackling sound heralds the stigmata of the drape

A shadow of a small, slender man makes its way
Across the picture window's roiling panorama
It's a picture of a movement, graceful, eccentric
Rhythm, a shade with a deep voice, and it knows

"Wake up, Joanie," it says to me, so unmistakably
Cadence kisses my ear with warmth emanating
From something that cannot occur. O Devil Wind
Howling beast in a burning furnace is a healer

The figure fights its way through the blow to a
90° angle of the outside wall; a knock, a fall
Something punches through the squall, very small
It leaves a slate-colored fingerprint that writes

The message left, in a precise florid hand reads
"Yes, it is me, Nathan. Your Daddy is with you"
As if he had to tell me that. "Yes, I know it's you"
He replies: "Good, I need to ask you a favor"

Diptych, or Josey's Boomerang
February 25, 2015, New York City

How quickly an illusion magnifies in the air
One moment, New York City smites the eyes
With stone, spit, noise, prosperity, depravity
Six hours later, plus another two by ground
The airbus touches down and then the heat
Scorches the bosom as eyes gulp up green

Bones toast, legs squeeze a moisture of green
Warm breezes nibble flesh, serve blasts of air
Opulent showers foretell of lush depravity
Feet no longer hug pavement, they kiss ground
There's no "there" there; oh, but there's heat
The dust infuses mouths and lungs and eyes

In concrete terms, NYC exudes depravity
A prime source of verdure is Bowling Green
No private moment escapes the public eye
While South California has no solid ground
Mountains, surf and desert vacuum the air
Culture-shy bliss offers pure ubiquitous heat

Imagine now a fictive place that covets air
It lives in the mind, it grows behind the eyes
Each blink smears waking thoughts with green
A trance may bring sharp cold or twisting heat
Familiar scenes brew comfort and depravity
Parallel bubbles, they beckon us on the ground

Whether we wake in a scene of sumptuous heat
Or ice chateau, we balance despite depravity
The conditions are concepts of hope, zeal and air
The sea laced in pink, the sky clad in lively green
Are raw minerals and elements so finely ground
They confuse the truth for transitory eyes

Thus travel divulges a realm of witty depravity
Envy dresses in azure blue and Persian green
Earth takes flight as an airbus plunders eyes
Flame chariots loom below on billowy ground
Ocean bottoms exude aromatic vapors to air
Ice islands sweating the spoils of summer heat

Forget hot swagger or chlorine pigment's green
Have no fear of vertigo, nor love of solid ground
Allegories of breath deliver light to lucent eyes

A Little Pianist and a Sleeping Maiden
March 30, 2014, Van Nuys, CA

Close your eyes and imagine
Hands, hands holding your hands
Hands held aloft in your beating
Heart; so the life that you have
In your hands is in part the start
Of an intercostal break apart from
The dart of images that swims in
Your mind when you close your
Eyes and hold the fractal barb; the
Prism of return will burn and for
All you learn as you pass through
Holes of sky and cloud, a comet
Passes by and life leaps to its
Right of way; a ventricle vibrates,
The vortex of the beat inflames
The heated cellular wall; now all
Is visible at last, fluttering past

Surviving Petrarch's Insistence
March 20, 2015, Van Nuys, CA

What have you lost, my child, since I am gone?
What have you amputated, or cast off?
What do you miss, my daily scent and scoff?
The science and pleasure of skin and bone?
The truth of moments shared with Debussy?
The laughter and the crush of flesh and urge?
The fire of minds when intellects diverge
When our congenial fabric wants to flee?
I held you in my arms when you were frail
So fragile I could break you with my will
I watched you grow to womanhood until
You held me when my body had its fill

You come to me again on equal turf
And so we'll dance again beyond the surf

Lilith, or DNA's Consort
June 4, 2015, New York City

All ready. Ah and so this is how it is
Standing on an embankment of a dry dusty road
Having gotten too close, too familiar, furry wings
About to fry to a crisp in the hot unforgiving dusk
How dry can the dusk be? Dry tufted brook
Dry crackling water of rank sweat, is there a well

The tuft is a mirage crackling at the fires of Hades
But this is of course before all that, barely after the
First try so hideous she was hidden (but only partly)
The first Adam was the only Adam because a man will do
As he is, acceptable despite all flaws and misdemeanors
Except his craven reluctance to submit to minor surgery

"No, Papa G-d, I don't want you to take one of my ribs
And give it to an unformed dirt bag...PLEASE!"
Papa G-d takes a long, sour look at this unruly golem
So uncultivated and innocent. He rumbles geologically
"Okay." So Lilith was whirled out of the dust to become
A comely woman; Adam issued a rather dopey smile

Sometimes dust cannot be accounted for; the whirling was
The first indication that something was slightly awry
She was perfect—from her exquisitely carved features and
Silvery laugh to her womanly breasts; from her honeyed
Triangle of Venus to her tapering legs and sculpted feet
But she whirled like a dervish when her wants went unmet

As unruly as Adam's shaggy mane of hair that she would
Twirl around on her dainty fingers, unless he denied her
Anything at all; then she'd twist and tear at his locks until
"Papa G-d," he howled. "What kind of mate did you send?"
"It is called a demon, my child, and has a will of its own."
"It! She said her name is Lilith, that she's my complement"

"Ha-ha-ha! She's made of dirt, exactly as you are
She's your mirror image, your doppelganger. You two
May as well be one." Adam wasn't sure if he liked that
"How is it supposed to work, Papa G-d?" He felt afraid
"Clearly it doesn't," he rumbled. "We must cast her out"
"Cast her out?" Adam quaked. "What? Where? Wait!!!"

"My Word is the word of Word" spake the Supreme Poet
After his summary judgment. Lilith was driven out of a
Quadrant which came to be known as Eden. "Some Garden
Of Delights," she said sourly. A hundred colorful birds that
Only yesterday sang and pirouetted on her delicate fingers
Transformed into Harpies in heat that defecated on her face

She barely had time to grab a cloak to shelter herself from
A storm congregating on the horizon toward which she fled
Lilith's sentence: Papa G-d unmercifully decided to send her
To a Theater of the Oppressed workshop in the West Village
To learn to be proper beyond humor—that old group dynamic
Had her in its spell; she was perplexed and paralyzed with fear

Ice Angels

Robin Dawn Hudechek

Named After a Bird

Dawn Robin or Robin Dawn:
you couldn't decide on a name until
the nurse cradling me
fragile as glass in a blanket,
placed me on your chest.

Arms flailing like wings shorn of feathers,
on the day I was born I was too tiny to hold.

Head bent into my chest,
and eyes squeezed shut

I wish I could have smiled up at you
before the nurse took me away.

No arms would spread like wings
when the only hands that could reach for me
were cloaked in institutional plastic.
I waited for you behind glass walls.

Eight weeks in an incubator.

Mom, I'm sorry I cried when you picked me up
and stopped crying when you put me down,
a bird crouching in the safest corner of the nest,
a crib lined in pretty plastic bars.

Mean Teacher

The Mean Teacher is coming,
the babysitter warned us.
Her fingers curl like talons outside our window.

The mean teacher is coming.
My father's belt swings in one of her hands,
a mini chalkboard, in the other.

The mean teacher is coming.
The babysitter warned us.
She will make me learn my abcs.
Letters bright as fruit plastered our walls.
My sister can read whole sentences.
Her gold star shines on her forehead,
but I'm too slow.

The mean teacher is coming.
The babysitter warned me.
My father slips his belt off his pants,
hits me hard if I cry, and hits me harder
when I can't stop crying.

The mean teacher is coming.
I don't want to learn my letters. I'm five.
I want to watch Sesame Street.
I want a life free as Oscar,
living in a trash can.
My banana peels will smell clean and sweet
and keep intruders away from my door.

The mean teacher is here:
the babysitter floods the room with light.
Hands arc outside our windows like claws,
naked hands without sleeves or rings,
a woman's hands.

The mean teacher is here.
She can hear the shouting and doors slamming.
My mother is crying. My father's fist
smashes into her face.
My sister runs from the room,
but I can't stop watching.

The mean teacher is here.
One day my father will leave.

But he comes home every night for dinner.
This night I will crawl into his lap and
and tell him about the mean teacher
and he will believe me.

The mean teacher was here.
No, that's only the neighbor. My father points
to a man red-headed as Archie in the comics.
It doesn't matter that his fingers are short and stubby,
too unlovely to distend into claws.
The hands in the window are gone.
The neighbor was never told
how my father protected me that one night
before he turned the key in the door
and never returned.

Flight

When I was a child flying was effortless,
soaring into the teetering hull
of sky, feathers scattering around me,
a silky down on my clothes.

Leaping from a schoolyard swing, the wind
would carry me, flaps of black swings dangling below,
tangling in a net of air.

Sometimes it was with the grace of a ballerina I flew
above our staircase en pointe,
leaping from step to stair up, down, then up again
at impossible heights, legs arcing
and toes descending to touch stairs
like hummingbirds dipping into sugar water.

When the sky was too heavy, and my Nikes, loosely tied,
remained tethered to the earth
there was always water.
I could feel my own weightlessness,
spread my arms wide above sea anemones
and light peering from the cracks of a coral reef
or an ancient chest shimmering with gold pieces,
miles below the reach of my splayed fingers
and the far too-distant sun.

Forest Park

Her fingers curled around the fence spokes
clinging to the threads of wire
as if they were kite strings
and she was borne on a cloud
of kites with long tiger tails.
She liked the way they whipped the wind
higher than a kickball that buzzed up, distant
like a bee hovering over flowers.
Watcha lookin' at, retard? Her knuckles whitened
around rusted wire.
She was close enough
to hear the shouts but not the voices.
At dusk, when children streamed past her
on shiny new bikes, she gathered kite strings
from the ground and imagined them
growing as wild as a dandelion's hair
but they were spotted, torn,
and when she lifted one
it would not fly.

Princess June 29

My birthday was the one day of the year
I felt special. It was the one day I was sure
no one would laugh at my bowlegged walk
cheap Kmart clothes, or the awful haircut
my babysitter gave me when I was nine.
When the photographer took the school photos
he gave other children names like Princess
or Peaches. I was Porcupine.

In those years I hid my stories under my bed:
comic strips with bubbles of dialogue,
wicked witches and fairies. I was ashamed
of these stories about June 29,
a fairy princess named after my birthday.
It didn't matter that my friends
and cousins all wanted to be birthday princesses.
We fashioned our crowns from tin foil.
Sparkling pinwheels became magic wands;
discarded sheets and beach towels were our gowns.

Barbie dolls became my characters.
The prettiest ones embodied the princesses
we dreamed of becoming, splendid
in their store-bought Cinderella dresses.
Before my parents gave me my first doll,
Malibu Barbie, I stole my sister's Ken doll
and put a sock on his head for long hair.

We never played house with our Barbies,
and I never touched my sister's baby dolls.
I didn't want to be a mother.
Our father left when I was five.
My mother, a nurse, slept on the couch in the afternoons
when she worked the midnight shift at the hospital.
No matter how many times she yelled at me
an hour later I would forget and run outside,
banging the screen door.

The kids at school never let me forget
I was poor or how ugly my special shoes were.
The boys chased me on the playground
and trapped me in the metal rocket ship.
Every day at lunch, a boy punched me in the stomach.
No one seemed to know how to stop it
not even the lunchroom monitor,
an old lady whose hand I clung to for safety.

Every week or so my mother made me
search on my desk and under the bed
for her missing pens. She never believed me
when I denied taking them. We never had
enough paper in the house. I filled every sheet
I could find with comic strip squares.
When the paper was gone, I wrote on the back
of discarded household flyers.

When my brother and his friend stole the bag
of stories under my bed, I flew at them,
leaping onto my brother's bed, an enraged panther,
hands slashing like claws. They ran,
laughing and waving papers inches from my face.
They had been stealing pages for weeks now
and reading them behind closed doors.
I stopped writing about Princess June 29.
A small part of me understood I didn't have to wait
all year for one day, my birthday, to feel special.

Ice Angels

In the winter we made snow angels
and built igloos from icy bricks
molded in plastic cups.

I never learned to ice skate properly
on sidewalks smeared in patches of ice
and concrete cracks that caught my blades
and sent me crashing to the pavement,
rubbing sore ankles.
I longed for a pond or a river nearby
a frozen-over world I could glide above.
Our snowmen wore the scarves
we should have kept wound around our own necks.

We loved the snow days
and the snow sparkling at midnight,
white as noon. No one watched the
clock when we pulled out our sleds
or crunched through thigh-high
snowdrifts, sculptured waves
settling against the banks of our houses.

We loved the cold hard panes of night,
the oak tree limbs chattering in icy cocoons
and snowflakes that clung to our windows
and slid down the glass, long teardrops
of broken wings. Snowflakes, tiny skeletons
of leaves, craved the warmth of houses,
fragile and clueless as moths
drawn to the heat of a brightly lit kitchen.

The whistling steam from my mother's
ancient teakettle waiting to be poured
into mugs and stirred into hot chocolate
called us back into the house.
We pulled off our soggy mittens
from nearly frostbitten fingers
and prayed the snow flurries and
sheets of ice spreading from street to street
like continents of moving glaciers
would keep us away from school
for one more day.

Wonder Bread

I must have been about eight or nine
when it appeared on my plate, egg salad
oozing like some sickening daisy-tainted lava,
a molten mass bulging from a pockmarked loaf.
I used to wish it was Wonder Bread
with its pristine whiteness and
oh-so-appealing softness,
bread that could be squeezed between fingers and
flattened smaller than a pencil shaving.
We never knew what was in it, what chemicals
bound its thread of dough. No evidence
could be seen of its molding or rising.
We only knew we couldn't afford it.

Our lunchboxes would never open
like desktops to fanatically ordered desks:
each spine squarely lined to the desk wall
each pencil in its place.
Wonder Bread was like that, and belonged
to a world of tidy certainties, of houses
with predictably manicured lawns, managed
by housewives weeding the sidewalk in a fury,
leaving no dandelions sprouting in hubbed cracks.
I could never understand
why rosebushes were tended with care,
while dandelions were ruthlessly
cut from their growing spaces.

We ate day-old bread
though it never would have been allowed
to take root in any self-respecting grocery bag but ours.

We ate what the other neighbors would have tossed.
I was too young to appreciate
my mother's pride in serving our more healthful bread,
whole wheat loaves toasted to perfection
in a deliciously warm kitchen,
the windows frosted over
so no one could peer in at us,
elbows shoving playfully, our much-too-loud
voices tipping into laughter, spilling into the room
like milk onto our easy-to-clean plastic tablecloths.

His Garden II

The rosebushes were landing places
for the windless flight of bees,
arched backs weighted on a petal
and antennae probing.
I wanted to startle them out of their business
and pet their striped bodies
when I should have been with you
crouching over the strawberry patch
and pulling back leaves.

You were proud of your strawberries
and taught me to search for surface imperfections.
Your fingers closed on the smaller berries,
speckled green at the base
and set them in the shade of the vine.

I would like to say I saved the things you gave me,
a ballerina whose crown was broken in the first week
and pajamas three sizes too big.
I see you in your alligator monogrammed tee-shirts
watering the lawn you insisted on mowing.
The kids are too lazy, too slow, too small
and when your car pulled up in the driveway—
"Grandpa's here!" we ran—
straight out the back door.
When we were big enough to push the lawn mower
you packed your machine and sat in the kitchen
for one last beer, then asked for refills.

Sometimes I hear the groan of the swing set
you put up for us, and our shouts
as we jumped from a bar as high as the garage,
careful not to let you catch us.
Then your voice in the hospital: Does everyone have a house?
Is everyone okay?
Behind me, ice blocks gather in the street,

leaving puddles the boys of your generation splashed in.
Now the ice trucks are gone, as are the
broad and generous oaks that crowded your street.
I look for footholds in your backyard
and reach for the low-hanging branches,
the heaviness of your stooping.

Moonlight in Your Garden

I see the moonlight in your garden,
I see its cold planes on your face.

I see the moonlight in your garden
as it bends over your grave.
I see your name on the headstone
and the year of your birth, fading.

I see the moonlight in your garden
as you brush off a dusty strawberry,
and offer it to my grandmother
who sits on her headstone
shaking her head,
hair spilling girlishly over her shoulders.
She's too tired for this journey.

I see the moonlight in your garden
as your elbow guides her through a thicket of grass
and your hand lifts hers, wedding bands touching,
and the moon illuminating your bodies
lithe and young as dancers,
slips behind a waiting cloud.

Bruises Like Flowers

Bruises bloom on her body,
this one floating like an iris petal
curling above her eyelid,
a warning blow given by her husband
the second time she salted the soup too much.
Her husband took one sip
and slammed his soup bowl to the floor.
Another bruise is a lily pad hovering below her thigh
where once the thigh was exposed to sun
and the eyes of men who saw her for the first time
in a bikini. She was so modern and stylish
she did not even look up when her husband
bunching a towel in one hand,
tossed her a tee-shirt. Cover up now!
They're looking at your chest
and she dared to peek below her sunglasses
at surfer boys with their laughing eyes
and Frisbees looping in graceful arcs above her head.
Maybe one would land one day. Maybe one would land now
while her husband was at the refreshment stand
buying yet another beer he would
hide in a paper bag and sip slowly
until his tension spilled over.
She would step off that towel
onto the sand and go with the surfer boys
shouting for her to join them.
She needed only a good wind to lift her
and a Frisbee spacious enough to ride in.
She would gather her skirts like living flowers,
look back at her husband shouting at her
from the open doorframe of the beach café
and never look back again.

Ghost Walk

We used to overturn rocks on the shore
and expose them to the belly of the sun.
I knew that some rocks should not be moved
but you picked them up to skip pebbles
and slice fountains in the sea
where they were lost
and you were satisfied
because yours had skipped the farthest
and the deepest
while mine grew steam in my palm.

Your hand in mine was sandpaper.
When you closed your fingers I was a bottled neck
with no wings flapping but the heartbeat
of one chipped stone against another.

In the ocean your rosary curls the foam
and the stones fly all in pieces.
As the seaweed entwines your fingers, I wonder
if you walked alone as you promised
and if the water sipped your lips.

Under blankets, my feet are wet.
In the moonlight, footprints pause on the shore
as if, in leaping, you turned. I imagine you found comfort
in the smaller hand that clung to yours,
in the transparent, almost unreal dress
that floated above her hair
then gave way, flattening against her legs
when you pushed her back.

Walking With Medusa

I walk secluded beaches,
my robes flowing around my legs.
Only here do I unwind the cloth that binds
my hair. Only here do I lift my eyes.
The clouds are as lovely and fearless
in their shifting colors when I look at them
as they will be the day I am released,
the day I am gone.

I would like you to take my hand.
Close your eyes if you have to
when snakes wind around your neck.
In their slow and calming hiss
there is love in all of their heads,
for the one who will pause
to admire the beauty in my face
my lithe body, my seamless walks
through forests. Take my hand, I beg you.
Walk with me. Talk with me
about the blackberries you picked
from the field behind your home.
Offer them to me in handfuls,
tell me stories of their planting and growing,
of the sun I rarely see.
Kiss me, cup my cold breasts in your hands.
Let the blackberries flow scarlet
from your fingers to my lips.
Close your eyes if you have to.

Impossible Dovetail

Sonja Johanson

Gabion Man

Like spillways, retaining
walls, filled

with smooth, pink granite-
glacial leavings—

horneblend placed by hand
in cages

carries the weight of consciousness.
A cobbled man

begins to stand, angled back
against

the battered coast. Marble
eyes behind

the windows widen. Penelope has
been waiting.

after Celeste Roberge's sculpture "Rising Cairn"

Lightning Rod

Who knows if they really worked? But
the farmhouse never did burn down,
so maybe. We heard the glass balls used
to be gold; by the time our family moved
in the gilding was gone—manganese
had turned to sun-colored amethyst,
and fewer than half remained up. Some-
times you'd find purple shards under
a rotting stair. Story was, if an air
terminal was hit the glass would burst,
and you'd know there'd been a strike.
More like, it was the neighbor boy
practicing with his BB gun, but still.

Still, I'd slip out the witch window
when no one was home, bare feet
gripping the asphalt shingles, walk
the low roofline to touch the section
rods. Even on a clear day, there could
be a sudden leader reaching from
the clouds, streamers rising to meet it.
I'd spin the violet ball on its bayonet,
seize the copper braid and swing down,
getting green on my hands, teenage
rush of electrons going to ground.

Hewn Beams

Each tool an analogue for the arm;
axe, because the hand is a fragile
thing, no use for felling and truing;
froe, that long iron lever, to split

and pry, peeling the log square; adze,
a turned head on the handle, a cupped
palm on the pendulum, the man a fulcrum,
standing astride, chipping the knots

to roses, taking it at an angle across
the grain to smooth a side for laying
floorboards, leaving the summer
beams rough to remember him by.

How It's Held Together

In any age, wood is cheaper
than steel, so it's by trunnels
that the frames are bound.
Gleaming locust, fresh from

the drawknife or spokeshave,
grain so tight it won't buckle
or tear. Enough on their own for
a barn or house frame, though

in ships they'll swell with water,
or be driven snugly by a fox
wedge. Trunnels cut flush with
the wall, or left out as a peg for

a barncoat. Trunnels pinning larger
things, fastening each to another.

Tenterhooks

First comes the clacking of the looms;
after the fuller has washed it,
cleaned away the dirt and lanolin,
the cloth is stretched on great frames—
a whole field of fabric, neatly pinned
up, taking in the wind and apricity.

Maybe it isn't such a bad thing, to be
stretched. Perhaps it straightens you.
Without it you might twist on yourself,
be less than you should be. Those
hooks hold you taut and ready. This
is the story we tell ourselves, as we wait.

Skein

coils of worsted yarn

a structure wound in a
continuous series of loops,

tightly twisted with
a hard-textured surface,

no nap; fine cord of
fibers, a thing constructed,

put in a coil, extending without
break or irregularity, happening
one after another, a series repeated
until satisfied; a constricted manner,

wound around, not yielding to pressure,
having surface roughness at the outer
boundary of the material layer, degree

to which the yarn that stands up from
the weave is present; minutely precise
line of twisted fibers wrapped around
this slender, elongated, solid substance.

For Jethro Tull

Scatter broadcast—
the tares planted with the wheat—
weeds so inseparable from their
host that they became the very
word for balancing the scales;
an accounting, a reckoning.

So many ways to improve
on that field of broken clods;
harrows—tines, discs, chains—
the teeth that represent our
fear of almost dying; seed
drill, to dibble and drop

in a straight line so we can
cultivate between the rows.
So much more food, but we
long to sling a sack across
our sunburnt shoulders, toss
these handfuls to the wind.

Jethro Tull, 1674-1741, inventor and agriculturalist

Spreaders and Weights

It is not in our nature to waste.
Every bud becomes a branch, every
branch might carry fruit, given enough
sun, given the proper crotch angle, if we
thin the clusters and the weather holds.

Faster, better, more efficient to prune
stray branches as they burst. But no.
We cannot bear to. Gentle-hearted, we
festoon the orchard, hang the trees with
bricks and sinkers, brace the burgeoning
limbs open as they begin to grow.

And when the harvest comes it will be
too much. Breaking under the weight,
we scaffold it up, we prop and crutch,
wonder what to do with all these
fetid bushels we never meant to raise.

Shovel

What you think you know,
you don't. The cards are wrong.

Spades are made for cultivated
soil, blades flat and square.

It is shovels that are pointed,
shovels that bite packed earth,

that scoop and lift and throw,
shovels old with rust that nestle

like scales on a spruce cone,
rachis exposed after a fire.

Misery Whip

Used to be, trees were so big
we couldn't see the jack
opposite side of the crosscut.

Now I could haft an under-
buck and cut the cants alone.

Splitting Stone

Don't be fooled by the grin
or that dopey accent—this man
can do the math. 26,000 lbs.

of Deer Isle granite, split
with a 2 lb. hammer, same
as the 19th century. He can

prop up the feathers and wedges
like ramets burst from a nurse
log, felled in some long-off

blow. He can play that block
of stone as though it were
a glockenspiel—tap, ting

tap, ting—down the three-part
line. The small cracks begin to
form; if you listen closely, you

can hear the faces starting
to shear. You can hear the music
of the hammer on the wedges,

the deep tones changing as
the granite breeches, the groans
and pops as openings reach

for each other. The hollows sound
as they come apart, they crackle
and pause, there is a pling of iron

as he pulls the feathers out,
silence where the stone
once was, but isn't anymore.

Foundation

Central chimney–ten
foot square, dry-stack
field stone below the frost
line is not enough to
hold a house together.

Even sill beams decay
with neglect: we shave
the doors to fit, shim
the windows, put buckets
where the roof leaks.

Floors are tilting away
from that certain core of
earth. The world is sliding
away from what it used to be.

The Seaman, Splicing

look at the doubt on his face
as he stares back from his photograph—

play-legged against the rails,
the coil of hard rope at his foot

his fid a smooth, long pin
the point just entering the braid

the shaft poised dangerously
in his ham-handed grip

To Sleep Tight

You must begin with a double half-hitch, and have all day, be-
cause threading stiff sisal around the pegs will take time, even
with two people, even if the tenons are secure in their mortises
to start out. Once you've woven the lattice, you'll need to turn
the bed key at every peg, pass and hold, until the siderails bow
in. You'll need to be shorter than people are now, and lighter;
you'll need to be happy with straw or husks or beech leaves be-
neath your back; you mustn't mind the way the mattress sags as
the ropes stretch, and rolls you into each other's morning arms.

Impossible Dovetail

Because once you have seen it
you have to try. You might believe
you are simply reading a magazine,

driving a stick, slicing strawberries,
but suddenly there is this perfect
puzzle, two pieces fitted that

shouldn't be, and you can think
of nothing else. There are no
directions, you just guess. With

only a caliper, square, and your
hopes, you score the ends. This
is your cross, but with your eyes

closed, you can see where it
might carry you. There are no
shortcuts. You have to chisel

out what you don't really need,
drill away what used to be the solid
center. Sawdust is everywhere.

There have to be cuts in the pins,
long hours soaking the wood,
boiling it soft and pliable. Then,

with your mallet, you tap—slowly,
gently—so as not to splinter this thing
you love, but to finally put it together.

Love Me Tender in Midlife

Ellaraine Lockie

Love Me Tender in Midlife

I was fourteen
and a Future Homemaker of America
When Elvis swiveled
his *Let's Play House* inhibitions
In moves that made Montana girls blush
from Miles City to Big Sandy

Brandishing a guitar instead of a gun
and giving new meaning to movement
His fence-free brand of bawdy
disfigured the flesh of milk-fed morality
Indelible marks on all
but the most proprietary complexions

Mine flashing Pat Boone flawless
above goody two-shoes
instead of *Blue Suede Shoes*
Straitlaced in Luther League straps
And protected by a preacher
who condemned Elvis as *Devil in Disguise*
His songs subjects of Sunday sermons

So he served a forty-year sentence
during my matrimonial
and maternal hard labor
Before exonerating himself postmortem
far from the convent of Montana convention
in my California midlife conversion

Where my unblemished body
has been tattooed by release
Indelible marks that appoint permission
to move in *Any Way You Want It*
When *One Night With You*
replaces uptight with you
And the rhythm of new religion
resonates Elvis animation
through the limbs of a liberated woman

Song from the Other Side

Arlo knew the secret
long before scientists conceived cloning
He discovered it in the guitar strums
and famous folk lyrics from his father
Toured the country with reincarnate rituals
Mouth-to-mouth resuscitation songs
that released Woody from his soundproofed box

But did he know how many
other resurrections he wrought?
How the first bars of *Goodnight Irene*
could recall forgotten renditions from other fathers
Like one who sat singing beside a bed
banishing nightmares and cooling fevers
With such nostalgia that the daughter
thought Irene might have been her mother

Did Arlo know how his lyrics released
those moments long held in ransom?
Before breasts budded
and fevers that became adolescent endemic
refused to be soothed by a song
And there was no antidote
for the parental paralysis that followed

Frozen feelings that
endured the test of time
While the daughter slipped
on them in icy dreams
Until songs from the dead
melted early memories
That dribbled out and down
her cheeks in a concert hall

The Spelling of Sin

I never heard her say she loved me
But I could feel like a straight-A
Braille student the word jealous
The wrong sex to come out of a woman
who knew a girl spelled trouble
In the words *other woman*
even before she got to school

The only advantage of a daughter
being the obligation of old age care
Anything before that was cause for discomfort
When every Sunday they both heard
the coveting Commandment spelled out

So when the hospice worker called
to say the mother had just passed on at 91
That she lay in peace now
right beside the worker
But that never before had she heard
anyone scream so loud or so long in pain

I couldn't see from two states away
any tears in the corner of my mother's eyes
Just the slight upturn of lips
Since hearing is the last sense to go

Home of the Brave

The daughters don't have bars
across their rented windows
I spend nights wondering if I
raised them to be careless or courageous
They say the area is becoming gentrified
So I've stopped winding the gang wars
around my rosary when I visit

I imagine hummingbirds
in the morning glory as helicopters circle
See Andy Warhol's tomato soup can
instead of a man plastered in red
across a car hood

The hate graffiti on pavement and garages
becomes art icons of Mexican/American culture
The woman hostage in the grocery store
on Sunset a part of a movie plot
Popcorn in the lobby when gunshots
pepper the place across the street

And now that they are buying a house
in an equally improving neighborhood
I finger the beads of worry
about raindrops on a leaky roof

Mother by Any Means

She's sitting on my bar stool
when I come back from the bathroom
Her hand clamping a cocktail napkin
over my cream sherry
Don't I know there are men
who drug women's drinks?

She glares across the table
above cups of green tea
Concerned over a man I've met online
A masterful poet who metered
murdering half the population of L.A.
A *maniac* she admonishes
And don't e-mail him your address

She's pacing the New Mexican
motel room at midnight
when I return from the grocery store
Where locally grown produce
overpowered me for an extra hour
She's unable to understand
the epicurean pull of sixteen species
of peppers with recipes honoring each
I'm unable to understand her panic
that I was impounded by something
more menacing than a pepper

Until I remember motherhood
when she was an adolescent
and saw herself immortal
Contrary to me now
who knows I could die any day
I elect not to allude to the
charging rhino in South Africa
Nor mention the motorcycle and marijuana
I'm saving for special occasions
Omissions kindred no doubt
to my daughter's when I waited up late
for the end of each date

Treasures Today

The celluloid box with a painted Victorian Beauty
adorned with red roses once held
my grandmother's Black Hills gold jewelry
It now sits on her great granddaughter's bedside stand

Touched by the hand of nostalgia
I unlatch the metal clasp and lift the lid
To see what jewels my daughter
holds dear enough to honor in this heirloom

Hint of mildew and red velvet lining
gone blush and bald in places
cradle a cache of sparkle foiled envelopes
They shout *Surprise* from labels like Trojan Mint Mingle

Pleasure Wave With Vibrator Ring, Class Act
Ultimate Feeling, Kimono Micro Thin
Life Styles Ribbed, Natural Lamb
and one with Climax Control Lubricant

Easily enough envelopes to equal
my grandmother's thirteen children
and six miscarriages

For the Father

You who forsakes his daughters
No, your blood does not run through them
You merely planted the seed
It was not a sacrifice
Nor even singular acts of paternal intent
Dogs do the same thing

It's their mother from the get-go
who gave up the bad food, booze and cigarettes
when she wasn't alone in her body
Her body that became their temple
Her breasts that bestowed offerings
to the small goddesses
It's her blood that circulates through
these new links in the matriarchal chain
Strong as metal that can't be cut
with the teeth of divorce

As could the paper connection you cast
Then scissored along with their self-esteem
Maybe you couldn't keep something
so integrated with an ex-wife who left you
Or maybe your second wife is Cinderella's stepmother
Who knows well how mothers
carry their children buried in them to their graves
Who is gratified when the first wife's flesh gapes
a little more with each stab of your rejection
With each inch of indifference
to daughters you inflict with desertion
Just like any male dog

Slice of the Knife

I didn't need Valium or Demerol to laugh
in the operating room
as *The First Cut Is the Deepest*
played over the satellite radio station
Followed by Frank Sinatra singing
You Make Me Feel So Young
Even though one nurse just pushed
three pills down my throat
And the other plunged a needle into my posterior

As though it injected truth serum
I wanted to confess
that I wasn't doing this to look younger
I'd been hell-bent to obliterate the frown lines
ever since reading my grade school diary
where the little girl letters spelled SOS
I tried to tell the nurses I was rescuing
the girl fifty years later

But Sinatra drugged me delirious again
with *You Got Me Under Your Skin*
And the doctor stopped me in mid-mirth
with two five-inch slices of silence
Stripped skin from flesh
like a professional mink breeder
Before stretching the abusive evidence
into the smooth surface of salvation

Moderation

Others envy my ability
to maneuver life
You're so disciplined, so secure
Never sabotage your diet
Or waste time watching TV
You're the epitome of willpower
A model of single-mindedness

They don't know I can't
eat eight ounces of ice cream
without consuming the cartonful
Or that one piece of chocolate
will put on ten pounds
before I can control the craving
That if I ever tuned in TV
I'd never turn off a sitcom

They don't know I couldn't
do the gradual ease off Valium
Even with a doctor who didn't
condone my cold turkey cure
And that I couldn't control motherhood
madness until I career obsessed
on part-time projects that soon
became full-time preoccupations
The diagnosis an addictive personality
Bulimia of a mind
that operates only in excess
Where the difference between
a feeding frenzy and self-control
is only one exception away

They don't know the fear
of falling from the elevation of extreme
You're so neutral, so normal
The models of moderation

You can eat eight potato chips
and flirt with a man without marrying him
You live in the middle
And you'll never fall off
They don't know that
I am the envious

Insomnia

Incarcerated in a cast iron cauldron
while burned grease of night dissolves
dawn's golden grain rays
Makes a mess leaving the lumpy gravy of day
My first taste of menopause
that becomes a routine recipe
A mind curdling muddy puddle
Thick and cyclic where I dog paddle
through the roux to places opaque
Terminal tiredness obscuring surfaces
Skimming memory off the top
as I devour Diet Coke, coffee, chocolate
And slump at the side of a road
en route to a sleep disorder doctor
Who's never heard of hormonally induced insomnia
Isn't interested either so discharges me for bad behavior
Returns me to the solitary confinement
of pea-soup dense days with an inept chef
Daydreams of clear consumé
evaporating in the steam of night

Day dances in honor of its immortality
The sun jitterbugging caffeine beams
And casting a ceremonial spell
as it inhabits the moon's body
Metamorphosis a midlife curse
My mind the medium with body begging
Valium or at least Tylenol PM
to protect me from a pagan rite of passage
A feeding fix for muscles that twitch like my cat's tail
attached to its torso poised in pouncing position
Both of us meditating murder of 2:00 A. M. birds
worshipping at the sun's altar
Songs of praise or maybe protest
at the sacrilegious subversion of Genesis
Dr. Jekyll's reconstruction of Let there be light
A deformity destined to self-destruct
at the end of my menopausal era

Still There

The white linen jacket
minus its one closure button
sits on the massage chair
There for the last six months
Procrastination has moved and returned it
with each sore muscle's atonement

I feel the fabric crisp as an autumn leaf
But I look straight through it
Ghost of a lost soul instead of the top
to a favorite summer suit
That has become a cushion for the cat

Today on my mother's posthumous birthday
the violet blue on the ice pack pouch
takes the shape of wild flax flowers
A pop bottle vase on a long ago table
After the flowers edged our wheat field
and encountered my mother
Executioner turned mortician
And always masterful seamstress

Disgraced as though it were her own
4H skirt that came apart
when the county fair judge lifted it
Staying up all night to re-sew
my Home Economics final exam dress

Today feels like the Fourth of July
as I send the suit to the dry cleaners
It will return intact with a button
Cat pee stains barely there

Anticipation

I like the not knowing
The span of time
that suspends in exquisite tension
When possibilities are endless
and optimism animates ambition
without ignorance deceived as denial

I like the not knowing
The span of time
after submissions are sent
And suspense is delivered
daily by the mailman
or by an electronic ping
Dreams of literary immortality
that stay alive in empty hands
or in the silence of hope

I like the not knowing
The span of time
since failing the mammogram exam
When statistics leave space for faith
Between fresh appreciation
for perfectly balanced breasts
And the scalpel that slices
symmetry into grave reality

I like the not knowing
The span of time
where he lives luminous in my mind
Wishful thinking and what ifs
with fairy tale endings
Before facts dim the delusion
or convention devours us

I like that span of time
The not knowing

In Bed with Edgar Allan at the Sylvia Beach Hotel

What woman would think the ending
could be so exquisitely executed
in the arms of Edgar Allan Poe
That he could be more comforting
than all those support groups
books, herbs and hormones
This man who understood loss, mourning
and madness better than any of them

Across the blood-red and black room
a stuffed raven witnesses the war
between acceptance and never-ending longing
for when life still bloomed and seeds flowered
A battle Lenore didn't live long enough to fight

My resolve swings as polemic
as the plastic pendulum with scythe above the bed
Insomnia sends me to Poe's bookshelf
Where I find a tortured prisoner
who realizes there is no choice but death
before he is snatched from its immediacy

And I am rescued with him
Anxiety lifts with the moon which spotlights
the bricked-over passage painted on the wall
Not even the tip of Fortunato's hat
squeezed from brick before his bibliophilic fate
keeps me from falling into the abyss of sleep

The circular vise of night
Hot and sweaty before the tidal wave of chills
An awakening in a pool so red and spread
that the maid will think abortion with coat hanger
Instead of a harbinger for barren
Or hell's fire flooded one final time
Cramps, craziness, leaks and stench
being what the raven meant when it said *Nevermore*

Each room in the Sylvia Beach Hotel in Newport, Oregon, honors a famous writer.

Autumn's End

Green alters to Grand Canyon colors
in age-old October chemistry
of New England leaves
Chameleon change of life
Like the midway metamorphosis
en route to old age
Where verdant clarity of youth
and variegated complexity
of early adulthood
combine in full spectrum
I see me and a multitude
of menopausal sisters
Our hormones sucked out
by nature's straw
Chlorophyll leeched from our leaves
Leaving ruby orange amber splendor
that has been there all along
Some of us still gripping
boughs for security
Grasping bygone shades of green
that shift to bouts of blue
Indigo depressions that clash
with earth-tone beauty
And become brittle with fear
of forthcoming winter
Others of us float gracefully
to the ground grandmothering
into sunset colors
Or cluster in commiserating piles
Watching the balance of us
blow carefree in newfound freedoms
on fall's final breezes
Gilded in sunlit brilliance
of acceptance
We blaze into the inevitability
of autumn's end

13 Moons

Daniel McGinn

I remember the moon was covered with dust and I used my finger to write *clean me* on its surface, and my finger was ever after covered with a fine gray blanket, as when you pull lint from the dryer.

I remember more than I can tell.

I remember heaven.

I remember hell.

—MARY RUEFLE, "I Remember, I Remember"

January

If I stop and wait stars will reveal themselves.
Even over Los Angeles, the sky
is still the sky.

Street lamplight and shadows fall
into the arms of stick-figure trees.
My life is in transition. I wait.

The moon wanders off
to the other side of the sky.
I turn my lawn chair.

Leaves crumble at my feet.
How can anything in the distance
remain so clear and bright?

February

All day long cool breezes blow
clouds creep in and hunker low
clouds fan feathers across your face
and in seconds you are gone.

It's almost midnight.
All I see is a brooding bruise
behind a swarm of clouds.

If you won't talk to me I have to guess
what you are saying. Not talking is saying
something.

I am afraid I will fill your mouth
with my own silence. Silence is where I hide
my self-loathing, my fears, and my sorrows.

March

I don't know what to say about this new moon.
It looks like a television rerun. I've seen this
moon before. I planted seeds and waited for rain
to come—it didn't. I don't know if the weatherman
lied or if he didn't know the truth.

One by one my used cars died and were buried
in junkyards, stripped of stereos
and speakers. Sing to me, be straight with me,
tell me who you really are, I will cling to
your every word like moss, like a baby,
like a leech.

My shadow passed through thousands of thresholds.
My shadow followed me down this dark alley.
My silhouette is stooped, hands raised above its head.
I am not ready for this. All of a sudden I'm stopped.

My wheels won't turn.
No check in the mail.
No reason for alarm.
Nobody cares what I do.
I can sleep now. I can sleep for as long as I like.

April

1.
It's been a while since I spent my time staring
at the activity outside my hospital window—
a seventh-story window—facing a parking lot below;
a window that would not open because nurses never know
when a patient will discover how they really feel.

2.
I took long walks down short hallways lined with beige
doors, walls interrupted by neutral art, fruit in baskets,
earth-tone landscapes, calm colors captured
in whitewashed frames. There was always at least one cop
sitting on a folding chair at the end of my hallway

176

outside of a patient's door. I never found out which side
of the law that patient was on, or what sort of secret
those cops were guarding.

3.
My constant companion was an antibiotic drip bag
hung from a metal pole. We took walks together.
The nurses kept moving my IV needle. One by one,
my veins collapsed; I was bruised on both sides of my wrists.
One morning a nurse missed the vein in my right hand.
She pierced a nerve and the electrical current pricked a path
up my arm and out the back end of my elbow. I watched my hand
puff up. When I could no longer make a fist I called for the nurse.
She was kind to me, she removed the needle and said I could give
my veins a rest for an hour or two. No longer tied to an IV pole,
I put on pajama pants and a tee-shirt, grabbed a five dollar bill
from the nightstand and headed for the elevator. I rode it
to the first floor where I bought a cup of coffee at the gift shop.

I stepped outside and looked up. I felt air touch my skin.
Have you gone without food for days?
Do you remember how it felt to eat?
Standing outside was that kind of good to me.

A woman rolled up in a wheelchair, she waited at the curb
with a newborn in her arms. She made cooing noises and adjusted
a baby blanket while an attendant stood behind her. A young man
entered the glass doors of the building; a Mylar balloon festooned
with flowers followed him. I tossed the remainder of my coffee
into a trash can. I also went inside. When I returned to the seventh
floor things had changed. The nurses began watching me.
The nurse who had been kind to me wheeled an IV stand
into my room. She silently pushed a needle into my neck vein
and taped the plastic tube to my shoulder, close to the collarbone.

4.
The plant was down so we weren't taking breaks. The bosses were
working us as fast as they could. Four of us disassembled
the shredder. We were smeared with sweat and machine oil.
We removed steel plates and stacked them on a pallet, raised
on forks to knee height. Each plate was one inch thick. The edges

177

were sharp and steel is heavy. We could barely fit four plates
to a layer. We dropped one plate at each corner of the pallet
until the four stacks were 20 plates high. I dropped the 21st plate
on the corner closest to me and heard the pallet break as twenty
greased plates slid through the air and collided with the back
of my leg. The top plate made a cut into my right calf.
It sliced a triangular flap of leg meat. I was in shock. I could see
my tendons. The company doctor gave me 25 stitches,
one bottle of pain pills and a note which sent me back to work.
Things went from bad to worse. I had nerve damage in my ankle
and it hurt to walk. My leg was infected and the damage was close
to the bone. I left that job. Now I talk to doctors, therapists
and attorneys. They ask about the pain, on a scale of one to ten.
They ask about my ability to perform my job.
They never ask me how it felt to stop dancing.

5.
The woman in the next room never left her bed.
Her door was always open, she had a lot of visitors,
on the sixth day they came and went, all day, a parade
of weepers. On Sunday morning, the bed was made
and the woman was not in it. The parking lot was empty.

I sat in my room with nothing to distract me.
I can only read books for so long.
I need to learn to sit and feel.

6.
Now I have time to spend with my dog.
She is always sitting on my lap, protecting my body.
I don't have to tell her where I hurt. She knows. Tonight
she is sniffing the air, keeping watch over every inch of lawn.
I stare at the full moon. I am not feeling pain.
I have a good dog. I tell her that several times a day.

May
(*I Licked the Moon and I Liked It*)
    after Katy Perry

My lips were sealed.

She was sticky
like the backside of a stamp.

I was a man.
My apples were ripe with lies.

I wormed a finger up the slit
in her long black skirt.

She was soft sponge supple.
She liked to let me look.

I wrapped my arm
around her dark side.

Her white hunger
fed the envy of my bones.

My arms grew long and muscled
when I was rivered like a snake.

She came unbuttoned
like a button
and she begged me not to go.

June

Today was sheltered in a marine layer,
we waded through a sea without shadows.

Today I made a donation
for the funeral of a friend killed by a drunk driver.

I watched a mouse escape from my dog,
I watched pink feet, a black fur blur
scrambling across concrete with its tiny life.

Tonight I saw the moon poke its head out
from behind the clouds
a black mist rose up like a cape
to cover the chin, the lips, the teeth...

Lori asked me,
Does the moon always show us the same face?
Does it sometimes show us its other faces?
I don't know, I said and we marveled
at how clouds had misshapen the moon's skull
until it looked dented and pockmarked
like it had been kicked and kicked repeatedly.

Feral kittens under my house began to yowl.
My dog ran zigzags
and barked and barked and barked.
The mouse squeezed her body
into a hole in a brick wall, a tight passage,
small as a pencil spine, then it was gone.
No light twinkled.
The moon turned dark as a dime
dropped down a slot.

July

You are calm, cool,
the ice that drifts in my drink.

I reach for you,
squeeze you in my fist.

You are bigger than my life
and smaller than my thumb.

The moon should be thankful
it doesn't live here.

The moon is far away.
I decide to go there.

I climb out of my spaceship
and do a zero-gravity dance.

I poke around the moon in a tin-foil suit
with my stiff little flag.

I have no business on the moon.
I stare at the earth, the earth stares back.

This is how it is to be alone.
I have no language to speak of here.

The moon is bathed in silence,
a silence bathed in light.

August

This moon is coming at me
like it wants to curl me fetal
and toss me like a wave.

This moon will empty my pockets
of questions I never knew I had.

This moon will leave me mumbling the serenity prayer.

This moon knows what I will do next.

This moon is a highway patroller
pulling my car to the side of the road.

This moon floats and shines like a badge in my window.

This moon points a flashlight in my eyes
and questions me in a deep voice...

How are you tonight?
Where have you been?
Have you been drinking?
Where are you going now?
Can walk in a straight line?
Can you tell me where you are, right now?

This moon is not playing a game with me.

This moon expects some answers.

Blue Moon

Clouds like train smoke puffing
one after the other are sucked back
into the night. They make my lawn chair tilt.
I sit and watch the slow parade.
The moon curls across the sky
in the bright tonight, the moon is beaming.

Clouds lit up, floating around, have no idea
it's the middle of the night. Clouds of glory,
impregnated with rain, swim like fish.
White dog on a dark lawn watches a cloud
floating in a wading pool.

Some clouds spin like cotton,
some drift like smoke,
some sprinkle salt...

My face was lit up like a cloud.
My cheeks were pulled like taffy.
I fell apart. My jaw dropped from my skull.
My head stretched wider than a crocodile's smile.
My hair wandered off in wisps.

I am like a songless bird,
a blank face,
an empty beak.

The moon stared directly into the sun.
The moon is blind like love is blind.
Maybe this is not the moon
burning in the bowl of Magritte's pipe.

September

The moon keeps staring at me

A palm tree pressed against the naked sky

Tires sigh on an asphalt road

A plane passes overhead shoveling air behind it

Hear it   Feel it

One white light   One red light blinking

It moves   it goes   and it's gone

Electricity hums above an alleyway

Phone lines droop between telephone poles

I'm still here

I stare back

October

Old moon,
the distance between us
is greater than us.

What I once felt
I no longer feel.

You seem so far away,
like something I never loved,
like someone I never knew.

It's cold outside
Leaves are turning.

My hand lets go of the string.
The balloon is rising.
Tonight you are lighter than air.

November

This week we arrived
at a work-comp settlement, or settled
for what we are going to get,
we are going to get one third of one year's income.
Lori is sleeping, not talking to me
except to tell me what's not right. She keeps reminding me
of close calls I suffered before I was hurt.

I juiced greens, did the dishes and gimped
around the house, accepting things
I cannot change. I accept what this is.
I had grown miserable in the position I was in.
I was not getting rich. I'm still not rich
but I'm happier.

A coyote was walking down the middle
of our street in the middle of the day
only yesterday. My dog started barking
and whining at the same time—a bark-whine—
there wasn't anything but a mesh screen
between my dog and the coyote. The coyote
stood in our front yard and sniffed the air.
It looked well-fed. I picked up my dog
and we looked out the window together.
The coyote appeared to be smiling
as it turned and walked away.

This afternoon I signed a settlement paper.
Lori retired to the bedroom and huddled
under the blankets. She stayed under most of the day,
only getting up once or twice to tell me
that she did not want to live, because life isn't fair.
She pointed out that the two of us
would be driving used cars into our graves.

Lori finally got out of bed last night,
right after the sun went down.
We stood in the front yard
and looked at the full moon.

It was huge. *It feels like fall*, I said.
Yeah, she said, *but it looks a little off*
around the edges. I accepted that
and we went back into our house.

Yesterday evening—when I fell asleep—
I was two inches tall, walking across
a six-foot by twenty-foot conveyor.
This conveyor led to the paper grinder.
The grinder was rumbling
but there was no paper on the belt.

I was alone in the plant.

I was certain I had forgotten something.
The equipment was up and running.
I knew the crew should be around here somewhere,
something was wrong. Was it something I did,
or something I didn't do?
I knew I was supposed to be somewhere
doing something but I just kept walking on the conveyor.
Was I supposed to be at the courthouse?
Then, suddenly, I wasn't on a conveyor at all,

I was in my maintenance cage
wiping grease from hand tools.
My boss started yelling at me like I was his dog,
Stay! You stay!
I kept looking at my toolbox as I answered him,
I can't stay, I have to go to court.
He yelled again, *When are you going to wake up?*

Tonight, I'm sitting at the back porch,
listening to the rain.
I've been looking for the moon
but the moon is hiding. She is angry
at me because I don't fight back.
I'm not angry. I moved on
and the fight moved behind me.
It's cold out here, it's raining
and I can't see the moon.

186

December

Lori said tonight's moon is a ghost moon. I don't know
what's true; sometimes Lori just makes shit up.
Lori lit a candle and put it on the back of a paper crane.
She placed it in the water and whispered a name.
Lori may be wrong sometimes but she tells me
she has the one true faith. She makes me nervous
and I forget my manners. I don't even think to ask
if her faith was placed in the paper crane, the lit flame
or the ghost moon. It's an old moon. I saw it late this afternoon.
The sun was up and the moon was up too. It kept staring at me,
sulky and silent. I could see right through its skin and it gave me
the creeps. The ghost moon followed me all the way to the airport.
It tried to hide behind a tree. I noticed it out of the corner of my
eye when I checked my bag, curbside. I turned to look into its face
but it disappeared. I felt a cold wind blowing up my spine
when I stood in yellow footprints and crossed my wrists
above my head. I don't know what these machines are supposed
to do about terror but they helped me escape the moon willies.
I walked to the gate where I sat in a chair by the window
and thought about Lori and the paper crane. The moon pressed
its face against the glass. It looked hungry. It had lost a lot of weight.
I walked the bridge from the terminal and entered the aircraft.
I put my carry-on in the overhead. The stewards put on a show
about what to do when the jet crashes. They performed right there
in the aisle with props and visual aids. I was sick to death of dramatics.
I began to fear the shape of the theater I was sitting in.
My eyes were closed. My head was dropped to one side
but I was listening. Then I dreamt we were spinning inside of a bullet.
The captain came on the loudspeaker and told us to fasten our seatbelts
because we were about to exit JFK. We began to plummet down
the runway and my legs started shaking like a puppet. I was throbbing
with the pulse of the room. When the turbines hit a high falsetto
we were launched into the sky. I opened the plastic window shade
and the moon was out there watching me. I averted my eyes
and looked down at the bay. There were ghosts
hidden in the whitecaps. I saw them swimming in the water.

Lori says that, in Korea, ghosts always occupy bodies of water.
New York City ghosts bump elbows with people, they look you in the eye
as they rob you of sleep. These ghosts must be from out of town.
I saw them, bathed in spectral light, they swam like jellyfish in thin silk sheets.
I wondered if these ghosts had ever been dead.
When I saw their wings unfold they reminded me of Lori.
When those ghosts began to burn I spoke her name out loud.

The Afterglow

The moon burns a hole in the lapel of my black tuxedo.

The moon breaks my heart.

The moon punctuates the face of the water.

The moon gathers mist and makes a halo to wear.

The moon is saying something sexy and the sky is getting wet.

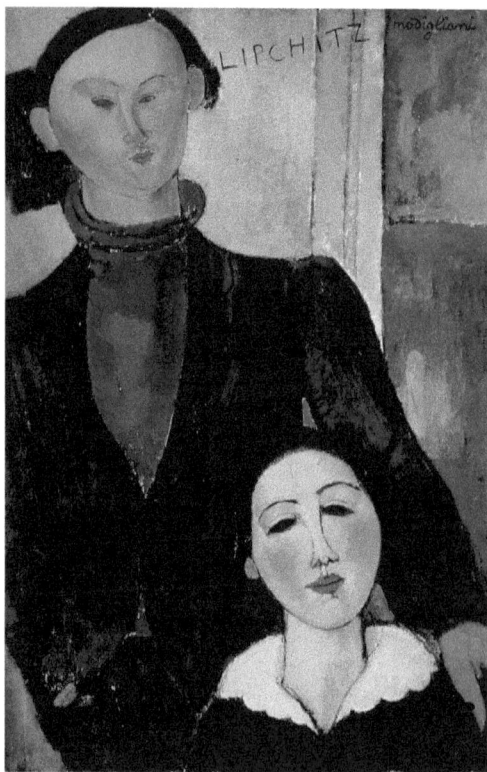

The Circumference of Other

Robert Okaji

At Sunrise We Celebrate the Night's Passage

And discuss not the darkness of crows, but the structure of phonemes
embedded in our names, the gratitude of old fences, of broken

circles and extinguished flame.

Two weeks ago he poured wine and declared himself Dog.

There are roosters, too, who cannot crow,
other speechless men, and lonely burros guarding brush piles.

What letters form silence? From what shapes do we draw this day?

Light filters through the cedars and minutes retract,

as the bull's horns point first this way, then that, lowering themselves
through the millennia, becoming, finally, "A" as we know it.

With my tongue, I probe the space emptied of tooth.

Barbed wire was designed to repel, but when cut sometimes curls

and grabs, relinquishing its hold only by force or careful negotiation.
Symbols represent these distinct units of sound.

My name is two houses surrounding an eye.

Yours consists of teeth, the bull, an arm, the ox goad.

Ritual

Placing the dead is seldom arbitrary.
The Marquis de Sade's grave in the forest at Malmaison
was planted with acorns so that he might be consumed by
trees, but my wife desires a shady plot in rural Texas,
where no one will claim her. In old Christian
graveyards the unclean were buried at the gospel side for
sinners. When her best friend died, she and his former lover
split a bottle of Johnny Walker Black and listened to Puccini.
The Nuer of Sudan place deformed dead babies by the river,
returning them to their true fathers, the hippos. After the fog
crushed Stevie Ray's helicopter, I played "Texas Flood" on the juke-
box and quit my job. In China, bones channel *feng shui*, becoming
part of the active landscape. Though she wanted her ashes to drift
in the Pacific, my mother's body lies in a national cemetery in
San Antonio. On the northwest coast of Canada, the Kwakiutl
left their dead to the ravens, and my father has proposed
on numerous occasions that we shove a ham bone up his ass
and let the dogs drag him off. I do not believe we'll follow his
suggestion. In old England, suicides were often interred at
crossroads, impaled, to impede their restless wandering spirits.
The Torajans sometimes keep bodies wrapped in layers of absorbent
cloth in their homes for years. I'd like my incinerated, pulverized
remains released in the jet stream, if only to escape economy class for
once. Jellyroll Morton's grave is in Section N, Lot 347, #4, in the northwest
quadrant of Calvary Cemetery, but some villagers bury stillborn
near a dwelling's outer wall. Hugh Hefner is rumored to have acquired
the spot next to Marilyn Monroe. Placing the dead is never arbitrary.

In the Key of Your Hour

The words I sing are draped in silence,
wedged between notes yet flowing forward.

Stop-time presents the illusion of interrupted tempo and meter.

Perception informs our spirits.

The old guitar hangs on the wall and seldom speaks,
preferring instead to lightly hum when the wind blows just so.

The conceit of two right hands. A slamming door.

Music enters my room by subterfuge, but exits boldly.

If simultaneity is relative, how do we assign primacy
to an overtone? One voice, one whole.

We must respond to our bodies. In kind, with trust.

I ask you to listen without considering the requisite commitment.

The broken circle represents common time replete with imperfections,
linking the measurable to the internal well.

Gather what comes, no matter the source.

Mark time and repeat: harmonics, the quivering string. Breath.

Self-Portrait with Blue

Darker shades contain black or grey. I claim
the median and the shortened spectrum, near dawn's terminus.

In many languages, one word describes both blue and green.

Homer had no word for it.

The color of moonlight and bruises, of melancholy and unmet
expectation, it cools and calms, and slows the heart.

Woad. Indigo. Azurite. Lapis lazuli. Dyes. Minerals. Words. Alchemy.

On this clear day I stretch my body on the pond's surface and submerge.

Not quite of earth, blue protects the dead against evil in the afterlife,
and offers the living solace through flatted notes and blurred 7ths.

Blue eyes contain no blue pigment.

In China, it is associated with torment. In Turkey, with mourning.

Between despair and clarity, reflection and detachment,
admit the leaves and sky, the ocean, the earth.

Water captures the red, but reflects and scatters blue.

Look to me and absorb, and absorbing, perceive.

As Breath Defines Constriction (Solar Wind)

The snake swallows itself, integrating the opposite. Or, illustrating the nature of earthquakes, encourages conjecture.

Wind meditation. The practice of circling mountains, of emptying oneself.

Matter accelerating away from the sun. The prickly pear on the roof.

The Tendai monks of Hiei run 40 kilometers each day for 100 consecutive days. Only then may they petition to complete the thousand-day trial.

Coronal mass ejections temporarily deform the Earth's magnetic field.

I sweat while driving to the store for cold beer.

The heliopause is the point at which the solar wind's strength is no longer sufficient to push back the interstellar medium.

No matter its destination, a comet's tail always points away from the sun.

At which point does one hear the sound of sunlight entering stone?

They must complete the thousand-day challenge or die. To this end, each monk carries a knife and length of rope on his journey.

A map is simply paper. Solar wind, cord of death.

Stones in the path, quivering earth. Eyes focused ahead.

The Language of Birds
for Lydia

Something thrown beyond
light: a stone,

words. The language of birds
evades us but for the simplest

measure. And how can we
comprehend those who live with the

wind when our own bodies
seem so far away? In the darkness
certain sounds come clearer, as if in

absence one finds strength, the evidence
gathered with every breath. Speech is,
of course, not the answer. We release

what we must, and in turn are released.

Rice

Yesterday's rain informs me I'm born of luck and blended
strands, of hope and words forged before a common tongue emerged.

Of my first two languages only one still breathes.

The other manifests in exile, in blurred images and hummed tunes.

Rice is my staple. I eat it without regarding its English etymology,
its transition from Sanskrit to Persian and Greek, to Latin, to French.

Flooding is not mandatory in cultivation, but requires less effort.

Rice contains arsenic, yet I crave its polished grains.

In my monolingual home we still call it *gohan*, literally cooked rice, or meal.
The *kanji* character, *bei*, also means America.

Representing a field, it symbolizes abundance, security, and fertility.

Three rice plants tied with a rope. Many. Life's foundation.

To understand Japan, look to rice. To appreciate breadth, think *gohan*.
Humility exemplified: sake consists of rice, water and mold.

The words we shape predicate a communion of aesthetics.

Miscomprehension inhabits consequence.

Threes

Difficulties arrive in waves,
lending weight to the theory of threes,

the plunging fund, a failed engagement, the self's
doubt, all combined to inflict the particular

misery of the ongoing, the continued, inelegant fate
that declares us human.

Look, she says, *the hummingbird flits from leaf to
flower, its wings beating 58 times a second,*

a fact not to be trifled with, for what may we duplicate,
contemplate, even, at that pace?

Say the hedge gets clipped, the ring whirs off the finger
and back to the jeweler, and all you know for certain

is that *you don't know.* There is no *why,* no *how.* No
way. Or life's reel unwinds and plays only in

reverse. Where do you stop and splice it, forming new,
uncharted worries? And what about that damned

bird, buzzing around your head in territorial fury? Yes,
yes, I know. These things are not my concern. Not really.

But they arrive in unending repetition, one after
the other, in clumps of three—lovely, lonely,

triple-threaded lines of vicissitude lapping at our ankles,
saying nothing, saying everything, saying it *used to be so easy.*

One Day I'll Market Your Death

Do not mistake this phrase for one contiguous with threat.

Even its flower knows the theory of attractive quality.

An ideal medium for cochineal production, the prickly pear
shelters a host of creatures we seldom caress.

Which displays greater motility, the cactus or the cochineal?

Life cycle of attributes, packaging, excitement, the unknown.
In the Aztec language, the word meant prickly pear blood.

The insects' bodies and eggs yield carminic acid, which mixed with
aluminum or calcium salts yields the red dye.

Reaching for substance is neither metaphor nor effect. Sessile
parasite: carmine. The product of *Dactylopius coccus*

became the second most valued resource in Mexico, behind silver.
Opportunism unveiling itself, revealed, or, layered greed.

What appears to be fungus is wealth.

One-dimensional / attractive / indifferent. We look together
through the window and observe our separate selves.

Window Open, Closed

We enter daylight in the shape
of praise, little words

billowing through wire mesh. Across
the highway a busboy questions time

and the concept of never, while
someone plucks leaves from the bay

tree and plans her day. Roger Bacon
longed to manipulate the inner essence

of inanimate objects, to harness their force,
and a lonely man swallows prescription drugs

deliberately, releasing their attributes over time.
My eyes redden from juniper pollen as the moon

spins invisibly above our roofs, tugging at the
clouds. I once traced in a building of music

the organ's sound to the woman I longed
to attract. Now, the window prevents the passage

of solids, but waves penetrate. I spread my fingers
across the glass, but feel no vibrations. Distant

sirens announce a procession of cause and intent,
of carelessness and indecision. Somewhere a voice rises.

Self-Portrait with Orbit

An arced path around a central point, bound to but held apart,
as in night's returning grace, or standing waves.

In periapsis, you reach out as I slowly withdraw.

Gravity does not prevent departure but prolongs it.

The acceleration of a body is equal to the sum of the gravitational
forces, divided by its mass. I rise from the chair but can't escape.

Not circular but elliptical.

Where falling away and curving from never meet.

Realizing that I am neither focus nor center, I discover place
in symmetry, in flow and subtraction.

A cloud obscures the sun and you close your eyes.

I wither at the thought of scaling or relative size, or your departure.

In the simplest Klemperer rosette, four bodies cycle their dances,
heavy, light, heavy, light, in a rhombic configuration.

My arteries fill in opposition to desire.

Wanting you, I absolve weight and listen, accept my place.

Wherein the Book Implies Source

And words form the vessel by which we traverse centuries, the river
stitched across the valley's floor, easing access.

Accession by choice. Inorganic memory.

Vellum conveys its origin: of a calf.

How like an entrance it appears, a doorway to a lighted space.
Closed, it resembles a block of beechwood.

To serve as conveyance, to impart without reciprocity.

Framing the conversation in space, immediacy fades.

The average calfskin may provide three and a half sheets of writing material.
Confined by spatial limitation, we consider scale in terms of the absolute.

The antithesis of scroll; random entry; codex.

A quaternion equaled four folded sheets, or eight leaves: sixteen sides.

Reader and read: each endures the other's role.
Pippins prevented tearing during the drying and scraping process.

Text first, then illumination.

Once opened, the memory palace diminished.

Self-Portrait with W

One might claim a double victory, or after the Roman Empire's fall, a reclamation from the slurred "b" and its subsequent reduction.

Survival of the rarely heard, of the occipital's impulse.

The oak's crook performs a similar function.

Shielding myself from adjuration, I contemplate the second family root, weighted in weapons, in Woden, in wood.

Not rejection, but acceptance in avoidance.

The Japanese homophone, *daburu*, bears a negative connotation.

Original language was thought to be based on a natural relation between objects and things.

Baudelaire's alphabet existed without "W," as does the Italian.

The recovery of lost perfection is no longer our aim.

When following another, I often remain silent.
As in two, as in answer, as in reluctance, reticence.

We share halves—one light, one shadowed, but both of water.

Overlapped or barely touching, still we complete.

The Sky Refutes East and West

Here, the horizon lingers.
The open eye, the mouth's shape.

A hoop, the circle without iris.

Does the screech owl acknowledge latitude and hemisphere?

The Semitic alphabet contained no vowels, thus O
emerged as a consonant with a pupil, morphing into a dotted ring,

and later, with the Greeks, an unembellished circle (which of course

they cracked open and placed at the end). The female lays eggs

on the remnants of earlier meals lining the bottom of her den.
If you listen at night you might hear the purring of a feathered

cat (the Texas screech owl's call varies from that of its eastern cousins).

The difference between sphere and ball.

To pronounce the Phoenician word for eye, sing the lowest note possible,
then drop two octaves. They usually carry prey back to their nests.

Screech owls are limited to the Americas.

Coincidence and error, the circumference of other.

Endurance, 1946

Unaware of the day's movements, she paints her
reply to the bracelet of light flaring above

the horizon. Tomorrow's edict is *gather*,
as in retrieving a sister's bones in black

rain, reassembling in thought
a smile that could not endure despite

its beauty. *I seek a place*
of nourishment and find empty bowls.

What is the symbol for peace, for planet?
How do we relinquish the incinerated voice?

Under the vault of ribs lie exiled words, more
bones, and beneath them, relentless darkness.

And whose bodies mingle in this earth?
Whose tongue withers from disuse?

The eight muscles react to separate stimuli,
four to change shape and four to alter position.

Turning, she places the brush on the sill
and opens the window to the breeze.

Exit the light, exit all prayer. Ten strokes
form breath. She does not taste the wind.

The Wind in My Name

Glenis Redmond

Dedication

To my family: Celeste, Amber, Julian, and Jeanette you inspire me to do and be my best. You are all my Sapphire Touchstones. A special thanks to my mama, Jeanette Redmond, you taught me about craft by first demonstrating mastery, while sewing and cooking for our family. Your love, patience, and wisdom have helped me to stay focused and encouraged.

To my Cave Canem family, thank you for the much needed fellowship and a place to develop my craft. Many thanks to my Peace Center Family, especially Megan Riegel and Staci Dillard Koonce by creating a space for poetry in the Greenville, South Carolina, community. Many thanks to the State Theatre in helping me to create a second poetic home in New Brunswick, New Jersey. Lian Farrer, thank you for your leadership at the helm and to Erik Stratton for being in constant support mode with a smile on your face. Also, a huge thank you to EMRYS for asking me to write my story when I returned to my hometown of Greenville three years ago and thus the poem "How to Make an Autobiographical Poet" was born.

A shout-out to Kevin Coval's YCA Summer Writing Intensive. It was great to be a participant instead of a facilitator in a workshop for a change. "The Wind in my Name" and "Apologia to my Double Ds" were birthed in Chicago. To my Alma Mater Warren Wilson College Family, thank you for giving me many different lenses in which to look at poetry.

To this poetic path in particular. Thank you, Great Spirit, the one that rules the Universe for having my back and for helping me to stay centered and not losing myself along the way. Thank you for my connection with the ancestors. As Maya Angelou says, *I come as one, but stand as ten thousand.*

To all that have helped me along on my poetic path, I fully understand that it indeed takes a village to raise a poet, therefore, I embrace the African phrase *Ubuntu. Because you are, I am.* For this I hold much gratitude in my heart for the village that has helped to raise to my present poetic height.

How to Make an Autobiographical Poet

*Griot Recipe
1 part father's daughter
1 part mama's child
1 part high-strung spirit
A pinch of being coaxed by sibling rivalry
A liberal dash of inspiration from those same siblings
1 heap of black Baptist preacher sweat and cadence
A dollop of teachers that spied the poet in you
Fiftyleven authors that spoke their freedom story
from countless books read that fell from library
and bookstore shelves
A Million Journeys taken inward asking *why, what for* and *how come?*
1 Cup of twin births old souls that stretched your creative backbone
A bundle of Nigerian roots extending across the Atlantic

*Griot: A storyteller, poet, or musician of West Africa descent that
keeps the lineage alive through oral traditions.*

Baking Instructions:

Be born to a father that played music by ear: gospel, blues &
jazz that rocked the family whole by night and day. His slim
piano fingers slid across polished bones playing music like
"Somewhere to Lay My Head" or Ray Charles's, "Baby I Got
News for You," depending on what struck his temperamental
mood. Stir in the vigor of his soulful songs, until they are at the
bedrock of your being. Set them so deep and firm that you'll
never question their existence. Understand daddy wasn't just a
piano player, but a true entertainer that held the family spell-
bound with lies, tales, jokes and, yes, poems.

See you, the little girl sitting at his knee listening to him recite
Henry Wadsworth Longfellow's "The Midnight Ride of Paul
Revere" that he learned in the 8th grade at Fountain Inn Negro
High School. Feel the marrow in your bones grow richer and
deeper verse after verse. Realize this is one of the many moments

that primed you to be a poet without your knowledge.
Collect all the music, poems, stories, and lies your daddy spun.
Know what he knew: timing. Play back all the Bill Cosby and
Flip Wilson albums that he played. So much so, you could
recount the lore and lies by heart. Mimic Geraldine's high-
pitched voice:

"I can stop on a dime and give you nine cents change."

Remember: Timing. Study your father's pool-shooting, smack-
talking and spades-playing mastery, which he used to reel listen-
ers in like fishing—catch and release—and the give-and-take
between words and silence

 Mix in your mama's stirred-by-hand homemade wisdom, a
simple meal, but feel how it sticks to the ribs, especially in times
of walking through the *valley of the shadows of death*. Watch how
that goodness holds you even today. Watch her by-hand agility
patch pieces. Witness how she multiplies nothings into some-
things.

Churn in that Air Force life: the one base after another. How it
took the family away from Fountain Inn, a life of cottonfield af-
ter cottonfield. Know even though y'all left the south, it did not
leave y'all. Know the red clay you could never shake, is in your
blood. Figure in this sense of place, though by age 12, you had
already lost count of schools, friends and kin. Libraries during
these moves were your one true constant.

Cogitate on this: how your gypsy blood got stirred and amplified
into a restless high-strung soul. Like Zora Neale Hurston, the
day you were born—traveling dust must have sprinkled at your
door. See how this vagabond *there but by the grace of God go I* atti-
tude has shaped your life. Reconcile how this made you feel,
always the outsider, yet resilient.

212

Taught you to never-meet-a-stranger and how to scan a map, as mama said, "like a man." Jump in the car, ride without a worry letting tires hit asphalt on some trips as long as from here to almost Canada. You have drive on top of drive.

With the gift of gab you got from your dad, you became a poetry evangelist speaking to all: from gated community privilege to bigoted beliefs to the backroads of the rez to all-good in the hood, finding at-risk heartbeats in all those places. See how your heart, like your poetry, leans toward the underdog.

Add the back-and-forth banter of sibling rivalry, the healthy competition of swagger and dance. Dance-offs and soul train lines with your brothers and sister—moves so coordinated that you all could have been called, The Redmond 5. See how your gift of written and spoken word evolved from this funk and precision.

Take the above ingredients blend and stir for 10 years. Introduce this child to Jackie Earley's poem "1,968 Winters." Let its black black black frozen in white snow revolutionary meaning catch you in a socio-politico hold. See how that thread runs through all your poems.

Two years later, see how Ms. Roberta Sergeant at Woodmont Junior High School put a pen your hand. See how you wrote and wrote in a yellow spiral bound notebook scratching only the surface of your angst, but your ink blood's had the potential to go deeper like the indigo ocean.

Warm yourself with these memories:

See how the ink never dried and still flows into grace and synchronicity into every moment: how you grew up in a subdivision named, *Canterbury*. Gotta love the Universe's nod to Chaucer. Understand how poetry has followed you: the poems of praise that you wrote for your junior high school friends came from blood memory; validated only when you took a DNA test that uncovered your Nigerian roots, Then, much later you discovered that Nigerians are the chief praise poets of Africa.

Feel the beat of the drum flow through life's twists and turns. Notice unbeknownst to you that you have followed the trail of leaf and bone, a path laid by your ancestors, becoming a mother of twins. In Nigeria mother of twins is a term of great respect. Kehinde Eghobamien, a Nigerian, says, "Twins are delivered to poor people to make them rich." Believe what your ancestors believe: twins are the bringers of luck. Your daughters Amber and Celeste your four-leaf clovers poetically expand your soul.

Remember your Bethlehem Baptist Church family that embraced you as its bard, at the young age of 12. Never forget how they took you seriously, so you penned poems for the married and the dead and spoke them from the pulpit. This, too, is why your poems strut, sing and dance and speak with the fire of a black Baptist preacher and expect *Amens* and *Hallelujahs*. Call and response: timing.

Go to Erskine College, be the literary editor of *The Review*, be the first in your family to receive a college degree in psychology. Counsel others for seven years. Your health slips. Find the shade tree of Julia Cameron's *Artist's Way* that revives you. Then, the circle in Susanne Abrams loft and later the writing meetings around Sue Inman's dining room table. Eat, breathe, and speak poetry 24/7. Get on your mark Get set. Write. Perform and grow. Introduce yourself to the slam circle and Poetry Alive! in Asheville all in the same night. See yourself crawl, walk, and then fly on a journey that built your poetic muscle to embody Willie Nelson's "On the Road Again."

Be gentle as you tend to your road-weary warrior heart, 17 years is a lot of standing in classrooms, on stages and writing on pages. Feel how it furls and unfurls by reckoning with Carolina's weighted history in verse. Get your MFA at Warren Wilson College to deepen your craft.

Finally, gain inner and outer sight to see not only your own hands that molded you, but also the hands of others that helped you to grow into the full height of your voice. Understand this: it takes a whole village to raise a poet and under these heated conditions of love and struggle: bid her to rise.

The Wind in My Name

No stage name no hip-hop moniker
'cause what my mama and daddy handed down to me
on the day before King gave his *I Have Dream Speech*
is grounded in what's real: Glenis Gale Redmond
As if my parents knew their baby girl born
in the sixties needed to be fitted with two black fist
Irony aside of the Celtic twist of the slave holder's grip
I like the tight fit of my two Welsh names: Glenis Gale
Valley on one hand, *Wind* on the other
and ancestral forces at my back
while I face the Shadows of Death:
the decade of killing into which I was born
King on the balcony of the Lorraine,
Evers in Mississippi in his own driveway,
the bullets that struck Malcolm seven times
on 166th and Broadway,
and mama's brother Uncle Pete
slaughtered by his so-called doctor,
boy take these pills ain't nothin wrong with you, but lazy
only for him to die the next day
on his living room couch at age 23

There's real hurt in this hurricane
So, there's no pretense just urgency
and I need every fiber in my fast-twitch muscles
as I blow past pain
as I run like the wind *in my name*
But they don't like it when we run
made laws against our legs poised in the arc of freedom
String me up by my given name
that they try to call me out of:
nigger, bitch, wench, gal, and ho
the noose they want me to work and twerk to
before I dance that swing and dangle
I got blood memory running
like a fever *in my name*
So, I jerk possessed with spirits unrest
to the cunning in Cunningham,
the slave holders that gave my great-grandma her last name

I got the silence of shackles of those that never rebelled *in my name*, but
they left the plot in me stirring with these *songs of freedom*
They say it's wind
but I believe it is fire *in my name*
My grandma rising up off the Rosemont Plantation
in Waterloo, South Carolina, where she stirred and stirred
but ain't no tombstone *in her name*
This ain't no play play, but for real
I try to keep it real even at age 9
Mama say, *stop acting so mannish,*
but you know legs crossed,
hair restrained like a dog on a chain
ain't headed nowhere: *and lower your voice*
because loud ain't lovely, but it's not in my nature
and if you expected it to be
you probably should have not
have placed the jet that broke the sound barrier
Glamorous Glennis all up in my name
Destiny and fate dictate I break laws of gravity

Black ink turns words into wings
that morphs into poetry It's in the teeth,
in the tongue, in the lungs
and the breath of how my people got ovah
Yes, wind, air, and the asthmatic breath all *in this name*,
but I got plenty of ground holding me down
geography in my name: Cherokee mountains
Yes, I got red *in my last name*,
the West Coast of Africa: Cameroon and Nigeria
I got black and green *in this name*,
slave port struggle *in my name*
auction block to sweet grass *in my name*
I got fire I got ammunition *in this name*
I feel like that female Moses
running over and underground *in my name*
holding pens and paper to hands and hearts
I say, *write your way out*
I Glenis-up everything: the depression
of my personal and collective history
Wind is a serious force not to be toyed with
—no cubic zirconia gleam

—no pretend in me
—no persona wannabe
just my grandma saying *all you gotta do is stay black and die*
and that that's what she did
after a 109 years *in her name*
I write what she couldn't *in my name*
I live and give breath to others *through my name*
I'm a force that breathes life into voice
take what my mama and daddy gave me *in my name*
grounded and rooted in what's real
I claim all this and more *in my name*

How I Summer
I feel most colored when I am thrown against a sharp white background
                                        ZORA NEALE HURSTON

I summer like bare feet on hot streets: uneasy.
Circa 1990 on the beach I am hiding
as always in the pages of a book.
I am a Sesame Street song gone wrong:
one of these people is not like the other,
one these people is not quite the same.
My heart is a bruised peach even at Myrtle Beach.
South Carolina is a weighted history that I keep reliving.
This photo does not capture how I got here.
I married white. I married into family vacations.
This is my first holiday at age twenty-eight.
Dressed in flip-flops and magenta Lycra.
I am black-and-blue collar uncomfortable.
I am from vacations never taken.
We played endless games of spades—
not going to the lake or amusement park rides.
We were in a tribe of *I Declare War.*
On school breaks we drank soda like water
down bags of Doritos and ran the streets
until the streetlamps came on. We busied ourselves
while our parents worked minimum-wage jobs. Vacation?
more like Vacation Bible School.
We made multicolored God's eyes
from yarn and popsicle sticks.
We were quizzed on books of the Bible.
I knew verses by rote: *God is our refuge and strength,*
and a very present help in trouble.
The Atlantic is beautiful, but troubled.
I am troubled too even when I know
that sea is a healer holding salt.
My wounds resist.

I look up and out and instead of water,
I see acres of land, black backs wavering
curved like scythes.
Field hands they called us.
Our hands are made of fields.

I am red clay and cotton
especially at the water's edge.
Back on the beach, I am overdressed
in my mama's *You don't have nothin to do?*
I'll find you somethin to do
The doctor says, *Adrenal Fatigue*
And *Learn to rest and breathe. Take a Vacation.*
Get a way and just play, but I haven't a clue
of how to plastic shovel my way out of this.
Build sandcastles for what?
I am busy digging with a purpose
Audre Lorde wrote: *We were never meant to survive.*
Everyday I nail-climb and knee-scrap dreaming
scheming of ways for my dreams not to be deferred.
Be Here Now, on this beach, but I am an empath of the past
White Only signs hang over me.
I am a black pearl ghosted by every bump in the water
Shark bite or jellyfish sting haunted,
but empowered by how my people got ovah.
My spirit knows millions did not.
Under the Atlantic they sit,
a divination of bones
that sing to me.
I come to the shore,
but I vacate nothing.
This summer is hot in me.
I am full of this past present,
an ever-present heat that I carry.

The Tao of the Black Plastic Comb

Bless my bad ideas and butt whippings:
the black plastic combs passed out on picture day.
Bless my taking the comb and listening
to the blonde-haired girl promising: *I can make you pretty.*
Bless me for wanting to be pretty,
but obviously lost in the whitest of seas
floating on a kindergarten raft with no sign of help
via a mirror or a black girlfriend to keep me from going astray.
Bless my Ramona the Pest ways, always getting it wrong—
collar and ribbon upturned always at the other end of mama's, *dag nam*
     your time child.
Bless the five years that I had already spent on this earth
those years already filled with my school girl sense of shame
wearing Pigpen's dusty aura like a shadow that I could not shake.
Bless mama's tug of war with each strand.
Bless my *tender headedness* that matched my heart.
Tender. Nothing, but tender—too tender
for my mama's heavy hands that did not know their own strength
pulling each strand on my head through the hot comb,
during this Saturday morning ritual.
Bless her command: *don't let nobody touch your hair.*
Bless my ears not hearing.
Bless the brewing of sorrow and regret that are already in my eyes.
Bless the back of the camel broken by the straw.
Bless my backside the day the pictures arrived home,
when my mama saw my hair as, what she called,
something the cat drug in.
Bless my eyes and the load they were already carrying.
Bless me a high-strung girl feeling like my family's punchline,
when they saw my first school photo each laugh felt like a jolt.
Bless how I learned to pocket the hurt in my heart.
Bless this act of survival.
Bless the small tines of the black comb: The teeth. The bite
that every hand is not a helping one.
Bless the little white girl that did not see my beauty.
Bless me for not seeing my beauty—
the years it took for me to unlearn self-loathing
and not one hair on my head that needed touching.
Bless this little girl within me waiting

to come back to this picture with a smile
seeing myself as cute and lovable
with sandalwood smooth skin and the deepest amber eyes
scrying already like a poet.
Bless my little girlself waiting for my return
to make the connection between then
and now: my hair now loc'd and woven
wrapping myself with both forgiveness and release.

Apologia to my Double Ds

I.

While other girls' breasts trained in bras
mine came here full C-cupped
not as girls, but as grown-ass women.
At nine, too young to carry the gift
grandma and her mama handed to me,
I felt only burden, not yet the power
that these backbone women toted.
Their breasts turned able-tongue men
into stutterers and stammerers.
Great-grandma wet-nursed her sixteen
and almost the whole town of Waterloo.
How my foremothers boasted
of their busts without shame.

II.

I was in their club, but I had to disappear
to walk down catcall high school hallways.
I locked and loaded you
into sensible blazers to block gazes.
The jeers made me feel violated
like I was showcasing stripper tits.
Mama's voice weighed heavy too,
they're the first thangs people see when you walk into a room.
I could not yet utter the word *beautiful.*

III.

My breasts, forgive me
when I could no longer carry you.
Had you trimmed to ease my back burden,
But you came back proud with the last laugh
like Grandma Katie
like Great-Grandma Rachel
taking a stand.

IV.

You ewers of homegrown milk
you fed my twin babies,
your headrests haven for lovers and children.
I see now as I carried you,
you carried me.
Forgive me my journey,
the long way 'round
into my own ample inheritance.

RSVPing to Lucille Clifton

> come celebrate
> with me that everyday
> something has tried to kill me
> and has failed.
>   LUCILLE CLIFTON

I got your invitation
& it was right on time.
Up off the couch I rise
from the doctor's prognosis:
You won't die from this, but you'll
sure wish that you would have.
Pinched by pain, I pray for release.
You say, *come celebrate with me.*
I arrive late to the party,
with my poetry shoes on.
I sing loud and off key
full-throated with no apologies.
With your invitation I take stock
of my *non-white and woman passage.*
You instructed me to make it up.
I do.
Follow your lead
between *starshine and clay*
Every time they try to break me in Babylon,
I keep dancing my dreams.
Shimmy the limbo
while I stomp on Fibromyalgia's head
shouting to this killing life, *you fail.*

*Fist! Bump!**

Daniel Romo

*Persona Poems

* a character taken on by a poet to speak in a first-person

* Spanish for person

Sin Titulo

You must not explore this feeling, it will pass. It has to. You must not
touch yourself when you think of her, or just after she has left your
presence. You must not tell anyone that she was in your presence.
Deny your own presence. Convince yourself this is not you because
you are not happy, anyways, and why live a life feeling like a caricature.
Drive to the beach at night and cry on the sand if you must. Tears mix
with waves carried away from your core. Here, you are allowed to touch
yourself. Here, you are allowed to wrap your arms around yourself and
pretend they are hers. The way she has held you like a memory you
revisit but never name. Remember the hint of friendship in her hair and
the seductive scent of her skin. Remember you are a man. Then write a
poem about this woman. Leave it untitled...just like this relationship.

The Body of Caring

You read that my eyes are distant orbs focused on suburban shores,
an act synonymous with self-discovery. Shattered masts stall
introspective visions and blur the line between *meaning* and *saying*
I am just fine. The proudest conceal the deepest wounds. Hide cracks
that began as simple fissures, never meant to sever an entire man.
I dream an armada raids and conquers me, sticking their flag
in my psyche and claiming it as their own. They discover loot,
buried in an uncharted ventricle, fresh to touch in a forgotten aorta.
No one walks their wooden plank; I want to hijack it and jump,
just to say I once flew. You know my longing for time travel,
want to meet me on the other side, want to reunite me with the life
you feel I deserve. You put a globe in my hands, hold me from
behind so I don't splinter, and whisper,
Spin...

On the Corner of 6th and Something

You say your newly painted nails
are black like your soul,
yet your smile indicates
you're lying.
Sneaky creases in the corner of your mouth
confide that it's more of a charcoal gray.
But the dark color scheme
conflicts with your hazel eyes
that I've taken to exploring
in search of a future
I'm praying exists.
We've tried to quit the beginning
of this relationship
as if it were a simple charade.
Release as if we were
pantomiming the art
of impossibility.
Because on paper we are nothing
but wishes.
But we can't let go...
and tonight we cling together
on a Seal Beach street corner
at the end of winter,
compiling mental items
on a bucket list
we hope to add to
each season.
We stand in front of houses
we'll never be able to afford,
and hold each other,
bone-crushing,
like time
is a currency
we're scared
we'll ultimately
run out of.

Supernova

You say you know what you are getting into.
That you understand the implications of
loving a man who has been hurting
almost longer
than you've been alive.

You realize that just because
I look younger than I actually am
doesn't mean I will die any later
than the average man my age,
his girth and guts concealing
any hint of waistline
and belt buckle.

You tell me to stop over-analyzing.
That aging is a natural progression,
and you will accept me no matter
how many eyebrows raise
in efforts to decipher the nature
of this relationship.

Because I don't look old enough to be your dad,
or overtly young enough to be your boyfriend.
Lovers in limbo,
though we know the direction we
are destined to take.

When we sat on the lifeguard tower
during the time
we tried to gut
our hearts from ourselves,
we stared up at stars that would someday die,
but not before providing sublime light
for billions of years.

And now we stand firmly together,
hand in hand,
knowing the glow our bodies give off
is enough
to keep us
living.

Tomorrows

We sit on the rocks at the end of the bay
and you say, People only come here to
make out or smoke.

Frat boys to our right who look like
Philosophy majors, light up and puff
and pass as if sharing both a discussion
and bond that extends beyond Aristotle
and brotherhood.

Feet dangle above a calm body of water,
and tears dive down cheeks because
you believe I don't want
any more children.

You say that I've already experienced
the natural beauty of being a father.
You claim it won't be the same,
that the joy will fade just like
the melanin in my hair will
before yours
since I was born earlier,
my someday-speckled grey
contrasting with your russet strands
while we hold hands and walk into a life
neither of us planned.

But you stare into my eyes,
just as big and brown and youthful
as yours,
and I tell you what your maternal instinct
has dreamed of hearing.

Reassuring words trailing away into
an April sky
swallowed

by a blazing sunset
    every
    bit
    as beautiful
as the one before it.

Fist! Bump!

I was a dog person and now I'm a cat person. But you say when we live together, we're getting a big dog. You lift your skirt and ensure somehow my hands cup your splendid ass when you want your way. And you win and I lose but I still win so I say, How about a Great Dane, Babe? We have poked each other thirty-nine times but still haven't had sex. I respect and love you more with each notification. The necklace I bought you with the two-toned heart is symbolic of something, but I'm not sure of what, just yet. Though you do confess that I haven't witnessed your dark side. When I was alone, I navigated through the murk and confusion with the aid of your emails. Glowing words that equaled genuine concern. You say we're forever when we kiss in my backseat and I have never trusted anyone else's words, but I believe you. When you tried to leave this relationship, you realized you couldn't disobey destiny. When I tried to push you away, my heart(strings) pulled you back. If we were dogs, I'd ask before I sniffed your ass and share my last bone. Then we'd look up and bark at the stars, as if we were destined to live a life of being constellations, ourselves.

236

Messaging

My thumbs attempt to keep pace with my
fantasies,
tapping R-rated scenarios onto my phone
as if the visions will disappear and seem
less sexy with each second
lost.
But before I have the chance to press send,
you have transported us from my bed
to a beach and then to the kitchen counter,
your texting prowess the result of a
generation of communication I've been
too slow to embrace.
Though I'm decades away from
Arthritic hands,
the gap between my response to
your romantic scenarios
borders between seductive tease
and awkward pause...

    and I worry,
    one of these nights,
    I will lose you.

Yet you have stuck alongside me
during my moments of hesitation
because you know my slow response
is never due to not sharing
the same feelings,
but a result of simply not being
as adept at expressing them
in the same way.

And you pause to allow me to
wrap us up in the covers,
interlock our fingers,
and describe a love
in which no timetable
defines it.

Permanence

We lie down and offer ourselves
like sacred souls and skin,
hands tracing over
stained-glass bodies
as if viewing masterpieces,
an initial act bordering
on blasphemy.

You fall to your knees
and put me in your mouth
to taste the remnants of every step
I've ever taken,
to trace the hows and whys I felt safe
confiding in no one but you,
and to ensure from now on,
you're the only woman
I'll ever empty myself into.

We are not accustomed to this
type of love for different reasons:
virginal harvest and prolonged famine.
Yet fresh sun shines on
our lives and bodies
combining to create
the same season.

I place myself deep inside you
for the first time,
each thrust instilling a trust
in which our bond may suffer scratches,
but never shatter.

Vacancies

You let them in your head
    and your body becomes too crowded.

Someone must be shown the door
    and the boyfriend's the obvious choice.

Kicked to the curb
    with an unwilling foot.

You don't want to believe their fallacies,
even though they don't know me,
but you feel pressured to say you think
    it's best that I leave.
    That I retrieve my heart
    and exit yours.

You asked for space;
    I gave you solar systems.

Whenever you've had hiccups that bordered on breakups,
    I was the one who held my breath.

Grip

I rub your thighs and the fresh smooth of your skin spoils my palms. Bestows a sexy blessing upon them I'm unsure they deserve. I feel lucky and guilty when I grab a handful of soft leg and ass, which contrasts with my worn, hardened calluses. Your body is a resort of the calmest rivers and streams. Mine is a mountainous mission of which there are no survivors. But I kiss your legs and leave a trail of my lip's remnants so I can forever find my way home. Leave memories of me across every inch I've explored. Then I close my eyes and hang on, as if ever letting go is even a possibility.

Liftoff

I picture how the kids mocked
your brows.
Ridiculed their fullness I imagine
that framed your face.

I envision the way they poked
fun at your nose.
Teased you for its width your body
hadn't yet developed into.

But when you tell me how your dad
got upset at you and your brother for
caving in his Honda's hood,
I can't understand why a dad would get mad
at his children for simply
staring at stars...

Today I hold your hand as you
ride shotgun in my car,
the little girl who has grown into her features
all the boys, now men, chase after,
as if I didn't exist and they didn't miss
their chance.
Because you are my copilot in life,
and we will fly away into the same night sky
your dazzling eyes
used to gaze upon.

Undertow

You text a photo of you in the dress and I say, Buy ten more just like it.
You shine like the material is made of flirty kisses and fire. My heart is
not flame-retardant and burns—like longing for a spicy food I know better
than to eat. But I can't and won't quit you, and crave you constantly like a
late-night snack. I'm no doctor, but orders specifically say to savor every
taste of you as if your body complements the finest wine. I sit alone in my
apartment and drink to your healthy thighs. Then I toast to your bottom lip
that I first sucked on extra-long at the beach, because I didn't know if that
would be our first kiss or our last. My fingertips memorized the contours
of your cheekbones while the waves crashed, signifying drowning or defy-
ing. And here we are. Coughing up seashells and wiping the sand off our
bodies as if we are a natural wash, rivaling the tide.

Dear

I hold the letter in my hands as if your words bypass my eyes and infiltrate
my skin. I collect your written thoughts to stockpile and give me goose bumps
when I'm feeling like less than the man you've fallen in love with. 😊
You wrote that I've given you that same smirk since October.
An eight-month slightly crinkled smile that was initially an attempt at hiding
true feelings I hoped were false. The waves were real but the undertow was
exaggerated. We couldn't be but we had to. That was when your arms were
buoys and kept me from drowning. You see me healing and I hope you recognize
the awareness of your eyes is partly responsible. You saw me as a broken boy
unable to mend and took it upon yourself to help resurrect a whole man. We
began as archeologists and uncovered each other's loss. Dusty. Alone. Untouched.
And we discovered a trail that led to a discussion, a dissection, of our daily lives.
Which led to a cave where we excavated conversations we'd never had with
anyone else. You love my honesty and the only lie I ever told you was when I
tried to deny us. You also love my randomness and my favorite food is bananas. I
understand I over-think us, and the future, with the 2.5 bathrooms we'll share and
board games we'll play every Thursday night; you point that out to assure me that
you're not going anywhere. Because you say someday we'll create a home and
start a family of our own. But you named your cat "Cat" and promise me "Boy"
won't be the name of our son. You confess that sometimes you look at me from
afar and that I make you the happiest woman in the world. And how I want to
make you my universe and swim in your smile and swan dive into eternity off the
fullness that is your bottom lip. You...Me...We have names. And no pronouns
could ever do us justice. But, Baby, throughout it all...it's always been You.

Homeless

Thomas R. Thomas

hopeless

shuffle stilted walk
you drift through
we invisible you

breasts bounce
in ill-fitting
cast-off clothes

blank stare
even you can't
stand the smell

sanity gone
stopped being
a woman

too long
to remember
stopped being

human
stopped
being

leaf house

she lives by
the freeway
with two
yippy dogs
straining at
the leash

evicted from
her home
the other day
losing her
leaky leafy home

forty-two going
on sixty-eight
she lives on
the guilt of
commuters almost
home from
a long day

she moved
her home
her perch
and vanished
from view

homeless

it's easy to misunderstand

to judge

to the landlord this is business
to the Renter—home, safety

the landlord has power
the Renter offends

30-day notice

...

they couldn't find a home
eighteen months in a motel
one month in—one day out

repeat

it's easy to misunderstand
how can you be homeless
when you have a job

Buying Cat Food

I see the
old man
with twenty
cans of
cat food
in his cart

"the dry is
cheaper," I say

he smiles

"they were
on sale," he says

"and the
canned tastes
better."

and rolls his
cart away

WIC mother
agonizing over
cereal choices

She, broken in the
darkness, draws fear on her arms
silent tears

failure

If you've ever

stood at a friend's door
begging for rent

and lost that friend

stood in the doorway
of your boss
knowing
why he called you in

forgetting to say
goodbye to your co-workers

written a check to
cover the last check

then had to pay
the fees to six
bounced checks

stood in the empty
apartment, motel key
in your hand

truck in the street
filled with
everything

wondering if you
will ever have
a home again

reached for her
in the warm bed

pulled off her
nightgown
felt her warm
skin next to you

felt her inside
soft and moist

knowing
she knows
you are a failure
yet she loves you

then
you
understand

Santa Monica Boulevard

As the homeless man leans against the wall, his bed the bus bench, nearby his few belongings packed tight in grocery bags, he watches the builders across the street as they erect a new office building, wood, steel, plaster, glass, and wonders if he'll ever be inside four walls again. He watches as the building grows three floors concrete slab to tile roof, his only entertainment in the day, and watches over the empty skeleton at night as he waits for the workers to come in the early morning to start their day, glad to be outside four walls—too confining, too frightening, too many ghosts. He slowly walks to his bench.

hapless

the sun is shining
through the blanket
shadows of the
leaves are dancing
in the breeze

he works himself
comfortable
in the slope
brushing the
woodchips away

wrapping the
blanket tight
around his
shoulders

he fingers
the empty
frames of his
old glasses
pulling them
slightly out
of his pocket

watching as the
passing cars
fuzzy in flight pass
in the distance

sitting in
his cocoon
world

a small bug
skitters across

his hand

he watches
relishing
the company

stares at the
dark blotches
on his skin
rubs at
the dirt patch

remembers
textbooks
classrooms
pencils
staff meetings
Deans and
sabbaticals

watching as
the feet and
car wheels
pass him by

Tattoo

standing naked
in the shower
she scrubs
the tattoo
just above
her breast

the wrinkles
distort the
flower of
her youth

and soap
won't remove
the wrinkled
image

the art
of invisibility
eyes averted
head down
mouth closed
stand aside
slip away

speaking words you say
it all in the space between
each word a silent

testament to thought inside
your head cannot contain you

shhh

don't tell them
he's autistic

they won't
understand—
think he's
a freak

dangerous

he looks
normal,
talks like
real humans

his brain
just flitters
in its
own way

shhh

Cameos,
appearances

A. Garnett Weiss

The poet is grateful to the adjudicator, chef, composer, doctor, engineer, friend, host, jewelry artist, librarian, lyricist, naturalist, puppeteer, teacher, and volunteer, whose life choices informed this body of work.

Maestro

On a walk, his old-man gait andante on asphalt
he hears a siren down the block
    A mother calling, "Davie, come in"
    The cathedral's twelve-bell proclamation
    Wind riffling pastel leaves of early May
He listens to his own, slow rhythms
Each heartbeat, each breath inhaled, exhaled

Words of an ancient poem come
How Jove and Mercury blessed long-lived lovers
    for their humanity in a dark age
    Turned their hovel into a temple above a flooded valley
    Granted their wish not to see each other die
Their limbs becoming branches
An oak, a poplar: Intertwined for eternity

The story stays with him
Words roll away like thunder after a storm
In their place, a single note, then a phrase

He turns the corner
At his front door, the phrase heralds a motif
The key in his hand

a new symphony

All that glitters

Glass.
    It began in the woods, by a slow river
    A sculptor with her eight-year old daughter
       digging at dump sites for bottle stoppers, bits of glass worn smooth
       or twisted with leaves into cranberry-coloured canes
    Treasures in the New England earth
Stone.
    The girl spent hours at grandma's, shaded by high oaks and elms
    She knew the gardening club gossipers, the tole painters by
       their diamonds, their chatter, the scent of the juleps they sipped
    To tame her mischief, these grandwomen let her play with old jewelry
    She'd come away with one or two gifts
    Bring them home, take them apart to find what made them beautiful
Metal.
    Her father tested aircraft. Took a seaplane to work
    Always repaired the family car himself
    She'd watch, hand him wrenches, oil
    Loved the mechanics, his tinkering
Beads.
    A shack by the sea, no running water, no phone
    A neighbor brought the girl a box of therapy beads
    She arranged them by shade, size, shape
    Made a first pair of earrings, sold for real money at a boutique
Wire.
    She met a lover amidst brass bedsteads in a basement
    Anti-war, she followed him to a country of polite streets in a grid
    She worked at banks, in TV; designed department store windows
    Held masquerades: Chandelier earrings, sapphire chokers—
       her only costume
    Later, other women asked for the glamour, the glitz:
       A pair of this, of that
Two blessings and a calling.
    A baby kept her off work, led her back to explore
       the shore of her childhood
    She discovered a warehouse of beads, brass, pearls, crystals
    With that bounty and what she'd hoarded
       she began to create for others

Design.
   An idea can wake her in the night; she writes it down
   On a black cloth, she places one crystal, the heart of the piece
   She layers metal findings of brass or steel, its spine
   Then adds handblown beads, the body
   A design can click at once or take ten configurations
   One pale amber teased her for years with a pendant's possibilities
   before gracing the throat of a dancer
Glue.
   She works in a warm, oak kitchen
   Thirty crystal suncatchers filter morning light
   A television plays old comedies—she listens, doesn't watch
   A jeweler's loupe, pliers, cutters, chains, fasteners clutter the long table

   Dollhouse drawers, small boxes and shelves line one wall
   Twenty pairs of earrings drip multicoloured tears from satin stands
   Necklaces, crown brooches lie pinned to velvet
   like a collection of exotic butterflies

   It takes patience and time, she says
   Each stone, each bead, each shape must speak
      its rightful place
Bling.

Beholder

He enters the library to a duet of caged finches
Thirty kids wait with stories to reveal
Let's hear you

The door creaks, admits the thirty-first child
Fine, moon-pale hair frames her face
  a patchwork of crusted sores
Her presence shrinks the room

She raises a rough, red hand

Fearful she'll sound broken
  like the cells of her skin
  he gathers his platitudes
  makes ready to soothe

          I'm Alice, her voice clear, strong
          I like to write—about ballet, music
          And horses: Oh, the way they run!

Inside Alice is a garden
  A field of flowers
  A concerto
  A stallion racing against the sun
    toward the finish line
  A beauty in flowing taffeta
    poised to swirl in a mirrored ballroom

He holds his breath

      Once upon a time...

After Gepetto

It must be odd...
  living with all those puppets
  you made

Though what you intended, surely
  when you sculpted their faces in clay
Added foam for flesh
Layered latex for soft, almost skin
Painted all in colours, true-to-life
When you clothed them in what
    their real-life models wear

When you spoke *for* them
  Your inflection, gestures, mimicry: Uncanny

It must be odd...
  taking on each character
  while still knowing who you are

Without a puppet in your hands, you blush
You speak with a gentle rush of breath
No harsh words, but no nonsense, either

So it must be odd...
Children, parents call to your puppets, embrace
  them like friends, like family

  without ever having learned your name

Down by the station

A week off from riding steel—
he doesn't know what do with himself

His great granddad, a conductor on steam leviathans
His granddad, a car man, inspected the loads
His father checked signals all along the line

Today he operates the train
Screens show a problem: he brakes
Unlocks a laser from its holster
Crawls under the diesel, its horsepower roar in check
Aims the gun, repairs the bearing
His decision alone it's safe to go on

He worked his way from brakeman
to conductor to freight engineer
Now takes passengers to and from a large city
Rests in a swank hotel between laps: a regular life at last

It wasn't like that hauling freight for twenty years
He worked nights, hardly saw his son, his wife

Yet he's wistful about midnight runs deep into parkland
Silhouette wolves racing across ice-glazed lakes
Snow so blue, so bright with a full moon—no need for a headlight

He shudders at his bone-breaking jump from the cab
Another train coming head-on, stopping within
a man's width of his engine

Still is plagued by the bear, moose, deer guillotined on the tracks
He turned vegetarian because of them, the mangled
suicides, the collisions at level crossings
He inspected the damage, reported the toll
but not on him

Where does it hurt?
    She doesn't know the answer at first
    A suspect lurks in folds of flesh or
        in the marrow of lies patients tell
        Their fear of illness greater than their need for truth

    She listens for the story
        in the drumming of the heart, the sighs of breath
        Reads between lines etched on a face
        Deciphers patterns in the codes of blood

    Loving science, math, she could have chosen engineering
        but genetics drew her to
        medicine's cornucopia

    She married a smiling man, worked Emerg. flat out
        until a child, stillborn, gave her
        pause

    She cut back, began a family practice
    Morning
        Coat off, computer on
        Patients, questions
        Examinations, diagnoses, injections
    Afternoon
        Prescriptions, referrals, reports
    No excuses if she runs late:
        Aren't you glad you didn't need my extra time today?

    Evening
        Home
        Two boys, two girls thrive
    Facing a snow-filled garden, dusky sparrows at the feeder
        she performs a ritual, asks herself:
        Did I do no harm?

    The many times she helped, even if she couldn't cure
        outnumber when she let someone down
    Still she wears her conduct in those few cases
        like a scar

A Player

Voice low, soft at first
he breaks into "Ol' Man River"
Jumps to *It don't mean a thing if it ain't got that swing*
Do wapp shwapp Do wapp shwapp Do wapp shwapp

One musical number overtakes another
in his relay with Sondheim and Bernstein
Rodgers and Hammerstein, Lerner and Lowe

Their scores become his intimates
he mimics their rhythms
Revels in their spotlight

The lyrics, the tunes, the storylines
play him like a rube in a con

Strip him of "Oh, what a beautiful morning"
Deny him "One enchanted evening"
Without their songs, would he fade, become a ghost
or find words and music of his own

By the Book

She inclines, a little, toward the kids, drawn by
  shelves of adventure and alchemy

She envies them, a little, their entrée into the
  theatre of words

    She recalls her first visit—
    a bookmobile, next to a strip mall
    Age four, she entered, silent and respectful
    Took so long to pick a book
      she was afraid the place would close

    She carried her selection home as a prize
    There, she dueled with her brother
    He loved history, she read stories
    They aimed titles at each other like bullets

Nowadays, she manages the library chain
Only has time to read memos and policies
Balances people and problems, expenses
  and expectations on her high wire

Once in a while, she stands at the front desk
Answers questions, checks out books
Practices a "shussh!" or two
Aware how her smile betrays her

All I can think of

To everything I say on the phone
Prue replies *I know, I know*

>A litany of sadness, lousy luck cling to her
>A loved daughter, always second to
>her beauty-queen sister
>in spite of skin so creamy
>when all of us hid our pores

>She married an Ichabod Crane
>He seemed okay
>Liked to garden

>Then Prue birthed her daughter
>Perfect at baptism, at six with a tumour
>while Prue was pregnant with her son

>Slowly the tall skinny guy went funny
>Wore leather and drove a Harley
>One October morning, left without a briefcase
>Said it was alcohol
> not a new lover that drew him

>Prue alone with her kids
>bought a house
>Worked hard, smoked packs of menthols
>Needed big black boots
>for crippled feet

>Then Alzheimer's swallowed her father
>She lost her job at 56

"Take care of yourself first"
I hear and hate myself berating her

I know, I know

What will it take to change her luck?
Novenas to some long-dead saint?
A Ouija board or psychic's consultation?
I'd try anything

All I've done is wish on a mid-winter star
for good fortune to grace her

I know, I know
that won't do much
but it's all I can think of
now

Crossroads

He   Blond, with skinny knees scraped by one fall and
another, the boy races ahead of his family through Swiss mead-
ows where morels grow   He's fast with a knife, its tip rounded
so he won't cut himself   Wants to be the first to fill his basket,
to reach the cobblestoned square where the village expert de-
cides: These are good; those are poison   He's paid by weight,
the Francs going to unmarried aunties who cook for men tend-
ing fields and flocks at the family farm   The women let him
help with the bread, the soups   At twelve he declares I want to
be a chef

She   Angular, tall in loose-flowing sand-tone linen, a
blunt-cut brunette wears little make-up save scarlet lips that
smile   *In my yearbook, I predicted I'd have a small hotel   People
would come for a fine meal, a fine stay*

Together   They exchanged countries and landscapes for
a while   He: Executive chef for an empire   She ran its bistros
Together, Janus at the gates of urban appetite   A holiday
brought them to the Fundy shore   They heard sighs of the sea,
caught the moonlight's minuet with the Bay, watched flotillas of
loons and pintails, asked each other *could we make it here*   At the
top of hill, they found an inn, its shutters scattered on the lawn
Steep, broken steps led to a wide front door   She felt its calm
It's right for us   They put everything into the down payment
Laughed off friends who called them crazy   Moved just after
April Fools' Day   Opened ten days later

Now   It's been more than a decade   She handles staff,
bookings and bills and greets everyone at the front door—a steel
mermaid, charming year-round   The kitchen, the dining room
are his domain   He picks chanterelles on their own 87 acres,
grows herbs to grace each plate   *You have to love and respect nature
To be open to what each season offers   The essence of one strawberry
can change everything*

Want Ad

"Required: person with compassion, patience, commitment. A willingness to work long
days, irregular hours. To cajole and charm. To organize and persevere.
Candidates seeking salary, salvation or kudos need not apply."

Lights flicker, invite patrons to their seats
Black-tie musicians file onto the stage
With the oboe's soulful summons
a concerto claims each listener

That's what keeps her on the phone, at Council tables
Pushes her to sponsors' doors, to host
Champagne galas, auctions and marathons

    She once studied civilizations found in fragments of pottery
    Thought she would become a curator
    That chance lost, she cried into cups of jasmine tea

    After she married a banker with the heart and hands of a cellist
    she brought three daughters into her world of caring ways

She canvasses house-to-house for the sick
Sorts food and files at an emergency shelter
Bicycles petitions up and down tree-lined streets
Grand marshals the parade to keep the orchestra alive

Prim in checkered wool, she leans back into
red velvet, her "to do" list put aside
For now, there is only the music

A *memoire*

She remembers each excursion for
        tundra mosses and lichen
For sea grasses and wild pea
Knows their names
        their scents and textures
Dries, preserves them museum-quality

Laughter lives in what she recalls
        as housewife, mother, teacher, student
As builder, birder, reindeer tracker

With her first step off the ferry, the island compelled her
just as the tides must answer to the moon

She returned each time more at home
Each time more reluctant to leave
    fields and friends, coves and cliffs
        Her talismans

Off and on, she mentions a man
Middling height, sea-grey eyes
A smoker, teetotaler, fisherman
Her worst critic, she claims

They restored a cottage by the shore
Hardly shared that home before
        cancer choked him

She lives there still
Never speaks of
    how he caught
    and held her love

Silhouette

'Xcuse me
>Straight, short hair. Streaks of grey.
>Navy suit. Boots, low-heeled.
>Three strands of gold at her neck. Diamonds on both hands.

She squeezes to the window seat, retrieves a stack of files.
Highlights in screaming lime.

The car lurches, lures her to speak above the clatter.
>*My grandparents, all slaves, came here "underground."*
>*My dad, a porter, started the union on this railroad.*

She pats the plush armrest.

I married a good guy. Had my first kid at eighteen.
>Four others after that.
>She worked nursing homes.
>Hated the body restraints, the conditions, the pay.

Co-workers asked her to speak for them.
>Sixty-hour weeks as their rep on shop floors,
>in bottling plants and boardrooms.
>*Never down a mine. No way.*

These days, she hears from bosses, workers:
>Can the person work or not?
>*I feel real good when a benefit's deserved.*
>*Sad if there's nothing we can do.*

>*Never called in sick in twenty years.*
>*I'm thinkin' retirement;*
>*want time with my new great-grandchild.*

>*Till I'm really old, I'll visit Vegas*
>*for the slots, the shows, the shops.*
>*Hawaii for the sea, the sand.*
>*The Caribbean, cruisin'.*

>*Been a widow all these years.*
>*Sure, I wear my new man's ring.*
>*Won't marry him, though.*
>>*Don't need to.*

About the Authors

JEFFREY ALFIER won the 2014 Kithara Book Prize for *Idyll for a Vanishing River*. He is also author of *The Wolf Yearling* (Silver Birch Press, 2013). His latest work is *The Red Stag at Carrbridge–Scotland Poems* (forthcoming, 2016). With wife and fellow poet, Tobi Alfier, he is co-editor of *San Pedro River Review*.

TOBI ALFIER is a five-time Pushcart nominee and a Best of the Net nominee. Her most current chapbooks are *The Coincidence of Castles* from Glass Lyre Press, and *Romance and Rust* from Blue Horse Press. Her collaborative full-length collection, *The Color of Forgiveness*, is available from Mojave River Press. She is the co-editor of San Pedro River Review.

CAROL BERG's poems are forthcoming or in *DMQ Review, Sou'wester, The Journal, Spillway, Redactions, Radar Poetry, Verse Wisconsin*, and elsewhere. Her chapbook *Her Vena Amoris* (Red Bird Chapbooks) is available and her chapbooks *Ophelia Unraveling and The Ornithologist Poems* are available from Dancing Girl Press. She blogs at carolbergpoetry.blogspot.com.

ANA MARIA CABALLERO is a Colombian writer living in Miami. In 2014, she won Colombia's José Manuel Arango National Poetry Prize for her book *Entre domingo y domingo (From Sunday to Sunday)*. Her work has appeared in over twenty publications, including *Jai-Alai, The Potomac, Smoking Glue Gun Magazine, Red Savina Review, Big River Poetry Review*, and *CutBank*. Every week, she writes about poetry for *Zeteo Journal*. Her poems and book thoughts can be read at thedrugstorenotebook.co.

JENNIFER FINSTROM teaches in the First-Year Writing Program, tutors in writing, and facilitates a writing group, Writers Guild, at DePaul University. She has been the poetry editor of *Eclectica Magazine* since October of 2005, and recent publications include *Escape Into Life, Extract(s), NEAT*, and *YEW Journal*. She also has work appearing in the Silver Birch Press *The Great Gatsby Anthology* and forthcoming in the *Alice in Wonderland Anthology*.

JOANIE HIEGER FRITZ ZOSIKE is an actor, singer, writer, activist, workshop presenter, caregiver. Joanie is a veteran member of the legendary Living Theatre, actor with and director of the dada/surrealist theatre company DADAnewyork and co-founder/co-director of *Action Racket Theatre*. Her work is published in *At the Edge, Dissident Voice, Heresies, Levure Litteraire, Maintenant, Silver Birch Press*, selected blogs and in anthologies, *Between Ourselves: Letters Between Mothers and Daughters* (Ed. Karen Payne, Houghton-Mifflin), *Have a NYC Anthology No. 3* (Ed. Peter Carlaftes) and *Women in American Theatre* (Eds. Helen Krich

Chinoy and Linda Walsh Jenkins, TCG). Her upcoming book of poetry, *An Alphabet of Love*, is due to be published by Barncott Press (London) in 2015. She spends her time between New York City and Manchester, New Jersey.

ROBIN DAWN HUDECHEK received her MFA in creative writing from UCI. Her poems have appeared in numerous publications including *Caliban*, *Cream City Review*, *Blue Arc West: An Anthology of California Poets*, *Cadence Collective*, *Silver Birch Press*, *Verse-Virtual*, *Chiron Review*, *Poemeleon*, and in a chapbook, *Ghost Walk*. Robin lives in Laguna Beach, California, with her husband, Manny, and two beautiful cats, Ashley and Misty. More of her poetry can be found at robindawnh.wordpress.com.

SONJA JOHANSON attended College of the Atlantic, in Bar Harbor, Maine She has recent work appearing in *The Albatross*, *Redheaded Stepchild*, and *Off the Coast*, is a contributing editor at the *Found Poetry Review*, and is the 2015 recipient of the Zero Bone and Kudzu Poetry Prizes. Sonja divides her time between work in Massachusetts and her home in the mountains of western Maine.

ELLARAINE LOCKIE is a widely published and awarded author of poetry, nonfiction books, and essays. Her eleventh chapbook, *Where the Meadowlark Sings*, won the 2014 Encircle Publication's Chapbook Contest. Other recent work has received the Women's National Book Association's Poetry Prize, Best Individual Collection from *Purple Patch* magazine in England for *Stroking David's Leg*, winner of the San Gabriel Poetry Festival Chapbook Contest for *Red for the Funeral* and *The Aurorean's* Chapbook Spring Pick for *Wild as in Familiar*. Ellaraine teaches poetry workshops and serves as Poetry Editor for the lifestyles magazine, *Lilipoh*. She is currently judging the Tom Howard/Margaret Reid Poetry Contests for Winning Writers.

DANIEL MCGINN has been active in the SoCal poetry scene since 1995. He's written about poets and poetry for *Next Magazine* and the *OC Weekly*. He's taught workshops for Half-Off Books in Whittier, The Lab in Long Beach, and the Orange County Rescue Mission. Daniel has an MFA in writing from Vermont College of Fine Arts. His book, *1000 Black Umbrellas*, was published by Write Bloody, and is now available at Amazon.com. Daniel, his wife, the poet Lori McGinn, and their poodle, Pearl Le Girl, are natives of Whittier California.

ROBERT OKAJI lives in Texas with his wife, two dogs, and some books. He is the author of the chapbook *If Your Matter Could Reform* (Dink Press), and a micro-chapbook, *You Break What Falls* (Origami Poems Project). His work appeared in *Boston Review*'s 2014 National Poetry Month Celebration, and can be read in *Prime Number Magazine*, *Extract(s)*,

Shadowtrain, Clade Song, and elsewhere. Visit his blog, *O at the Edges,* at robertokaji.com.

GLENIS REDMOND lives in both Charlotte, North Carolina, and Greenville, South Carolina. She considers herself Bi-Carolinian. She travels the country as a Road Poet with two posts as the Poet-in-Residence at The Peace Center for the Performing Arts in Greenville, South Carolina, and at the State Theatre in New Brunswick, New Jersey. She has served as the Mentor Poet for the National Student Poets Program. In both 2014 and 2015 she has prepared student poets to read at the Library of Congress, the Department of Education, and for the First Lady, Michelle Obama, at The White House. Glenis is a Cave Canem Fellow and a North Carolina Literary Fellowship Recipient and a Kennedy Center Teaching Artist. She helped create the first Writer-in-Residence at the Carl Sandburg Home National Historic Site in Flat Rock, North Carolina. Glenis is also a full-time road poet, performing and teaching poetry across the country. She believes that poetry is a healer. She can be found across America in the trenches applying pressure to those in need, one poem at a time.

DANIEL ROMO is the author of *Romancing Gravity* (Silver Birch Press, 2013) and *When Kerosene's Involved* (Mojave River Press, 2014). More of his work can be found at danielromo.net.

THOMAS R. THOMAS publishes the small press Arroyo Seco Press. Publications include *Carnival, Pipe Dream, Bank Heavy Press, Chiron Review, Electric Windmill, Marco Polo,* and *Silver Birch Press.* His books are *Scorpio* (Carnival), *Five Lines* (World Parade Books), and *the art of invisibility* (Dark Heart Press). His website is thomasrthomas.org.

A. GARNETT WEISS is an Ottawa-based poet whose work has been published in anthologies and chapbooks, online, and in local and national media, using the pseudonym A. Garnett Weiss or under her own name, JC Sulzenko. (Recent highlights: appearing on *Arc Poetry Magazine's* 2014 Poem of the Year shortlist, in *Vallum: Contemporary Poetry,* and in three Silver Birch Press series.) She served as poet-mentor for The Gryphon Trio's "Listen up! Ottawa" project, sits on the selection board for *Bywords,* and is inaugural curator for *The Glebe Report's* "Poetry Quarter." Her books for families and children include *Fat poems tall poems long poems small* and *What my Grandma means to say,* launched at The Ottawa International Writers Festival. For more about her work, visit www.agarnettweiss.com.

Acknowledgments

JEFFREY C. ALFIER: "Jezebel Drafts a Dispatch to Ahab on the End of His Reign" in *Conclave*; "The Soldier Willie McCausland Speaks of the Dancer He Can't Take Home" in *Iota* (UK); "Ranchero;" and "What Sings Through Hostel Walls on Carondelet" in *Main Street Rag*; "Waking Late for the Night Shift" in *Mosaic*; "Late Trains at Landstuhl" in *Penumbra*; "West Long Beach Littoral for Late April" in *Raleigh Review*; "Memorial Day Eve" in *Red River Review*; "Blue Notes for Fireball Whiskey & Ginger Ale" in *Suisan Valley Review*.

TOBI ALFIER: "Once the Dues are Paid" in *Connecticut River Review*; "The Tall One" in *East Coast Literary Review*; "Plum Trees and Women Next to the Applejack Tavern" in *Front Porch Review*; "In Flight" in *I-70 Review*; "Our Town" in *Illya's Honey*; "The Astronomer Measures the Distance to Living" in *Talking River*; "On the Perimeter of the Packard Plant" in *Pirene's Fountain*; "Papa and the Glow of Mariachi" in POEM; "The Angry Goddess of East-Coast Weather" in *Saranac Review*, "Cape Split" in *Sterling Magazine*; "Far West Texas" in *Suisun Valley Review*.

CAROL BERG: "First Self-Portrait," "Self-Portrait as Beet," and "Self-Portrait as Insomnia" in *Yew Journal*,; "Self-Portrait as Farmer's Market" in *Escape Into Life*; "Self-Portrait as Wife as House as Housewife," "Self-Portrait as Dangerous When Down," and "Self-Portrait as Book of Self-Portraits" in *Silver Birch Press*; "The Apple Speaks" in *Labletter*; "Portrait With Yeast" in *IthacaLit*; "Self-Portrait as Waterworld" in *Jet Fuel Review*; "Self-Portrait as Dragonfly" in *IthacaLit*; "Self-Portrait as a Glass of Chardonnay" in *Pirene's Fountain*; "Self Portrait as Bumblebee Knocked Between Your Bare Thighs" in *YB Poetry*; "Self-Portrait as Seer" in *Jet Fuel Review*; "Small Portrait" in *Blossombones*.

ANA MARIA CABALLERO: "Timing" in *A Literation Magazine*; "The Public" in *Big River Poetry Review*; "Said and Done" in *Silver Birch Press*; "Gradual Rot" in *Ghost House Review*; "A Notion of Marriage" in *Actuary Lit*; "Paco" in *Smoking Glue Gun Magazine*; "Yellow Tomatoes" in *Pea River Review*.

JENNIFER FINSTROM: "Daphne and Apollo" in *Connecticut River Review*; "Circe in the Upper Peninsula," "The Fates," "Hermes, Hades, and Persephone in Fullerton Hall," "Prophetess" in *Eclectica Magazine*; "Almost Sonnet Written While Considering Annotations I've Made in an Old Copy of Euripides' Medea" in NEAT; "Ariadne" and "Naxos" in *Primavera*; "Minotaur" in RHINO; "Almost Sonnet Written While Thinking about First Love, Greek Mythology, and *The Great Gatsby*," "Some Poems Are Spells," "Upon Revisiting the Account of Daphne and Apollo in My Grandmother's Copy of Bulfinch's The Age of Fable" in *Silver Birch Press*; "Missing the Stars" in *Tar River Poetry*.

JOANIE HIEGER FRITZ ZOSKIE: "Amputees" in *Levure Literraire Vol. VII, At the Edge Vol. 3*, and *CrocknBunk.com*; "Judith Malina" in Academia.com.

ROBIN DAWN HUDECHEK: "Named After a Bird," "Ice Angels," "Princess June 29," and "Walking With Medusa" in *Silver Birch Press*; "Walking With Medusa" featured on the Freshly Pressed site by the editors of Wordpress.com; "Mean Teacher" forthcoming in *Chiron Review* (printed with the permission of the publisher); "Forest Park" in *Cadence Collective* and in *The Ear: Irvine Valley College's Literary Magazine, Volume 19*; "Wonder Bread" in *Gutters and Alleyways: Perspectives on Poverty and Struggle*; "His Garden II" in *Incidental Buildings & Accidental Beauty: An Anthology of Orange County Long Beach Poets*; "Moonlight in Your Garden" in *Hedgerow: A Journal of Small Poems*; "Bruises Like Flowers" in *The Camel Saloon*; "Ghost Walk" in *Cadence Collective, Blue Arc West: An Anthology of California Poets*, and *Ghost Walk* (The Inevitable Press, 1997).

SONJA JOHANSON: "Tenterhooks," "Splitting Stone," and " Impossible Dovetail" in *Off the Coast*; "Misery Whip" in *Plum Tree Tavern*.

ELLARAINE LOCKIE: "Love Me Tender in Midlife" in *Quay*; "Music in the Air" in *Outrider Press*; "Song From the Other Side" in *Jukebox Junction USA Special Edition* (Lilly Press) and *San Gabriel Valley Poetry Quarterly*; "The Spelling of Sin" in *Taproot Literary Review*; "Home of the Brave" in *Ibbetson Street Lummox*, and *Minotaur*; "Mother by Any Means" in *Chiron Review, Thunder Sandwich, Free Verse*, and *A Long and Winding Road*; "Treasures Today" in *Chiron Review, San Gabriel Valley Quarterly, Lucidity*, and *Pegasus*; "For the Father" in *Chiron Review*; "Slice of the Knife" in *Presa*; "Moderation" in *The Year's Best Poetry* (Tickled by Thunder), *Lummox*, and *Target Audience Magazine*; "Insomnia" in *Fireweed: A Feminist Quarterly of Writing, Politics, Art and Culture* (Canada); "Still There" in *Presa*; "Anticipation" in *California Quarterly* and PoetryMagazine.com; "In Bed with Edgar Allan at the Sylvia Beach Hotel" in *Oregon Writers Colony Colonygram, Blue Moon Literary Review*, and *Pasque Petals*; "Autumn's End" in *Arizona Literary Magazine, Numbat*, and *Creekwalker*, and *The Mountain* (Outrider Press).

DANIEL MCGINN: "January" in *Avoid Ninja Stars*; "April" in *Cadence Collective* and *Drunk in a Midnight Choir*; "November" in *Gutters and Alleyways: Perspectives on Poverty and Struggle*.

ROBERT OKAJI: "At Sunrise We Celebrate the Night's Passage" and "The Sky Refutes East and West" in *Prime Number Magazine*; "Ritual" in *Middle Gray*; "Self-Portrait with Blue" and "Self-Portrait with W" in *Silver Birch Press*; "Rice" in *Heron Clan III*; "Threes" in *Eclectica*; "One Day I'll Market Your Death" in *Otoliths*; "Window Open, Closed" in Bonnie McClellan's Weblog; "Wherein the Book Implies Source" in *Boston Review*.

GLENIS REDMOND: "How to Make an Autobiographical Poet" in *Emrys*; "The Wind in My Name," "How I Summer," "The Tao of the Black Plastic Comb," and "RSVPing to Lucille Clifton" in *Silver Birch Press*; "Apologia to my Double Ds" in *Toe Good Poetry*.

DANIEL ROMO: "Undertow" in *The Fat Damsel*; "The Body of Caring" in *Altpoetics*.

THOMAS R. THOMAS: "the art & homeless" in *the art of invisibility* (Dark Heart Press).

A. GARNETT WEISS: "Maestro" and "Beholder" in *Maple Tree Literary Supplement*; "After Gepetto," "Where does it hurt?," "All I can think of," and "By the Book" in *The Saving Bannister Anthology*; "A memoire" presented at the Grand Manan Museum.

www.ingramcontent.com/pod-product-compliance
Lightning Source LLC
Chambersburg PA
CBHW060009050426

42448CB00012B/2670